D1401731

The Principles of Language-study

LANGUAGE AND LANGUAGE LEARNING

General Editors: R. MACKIN   PETER STREVENS

The
principles of
language-study

HAROLD E. PALMER

London
OXFORD UNIVERSITY PRESS

Oxford University Press, Ely House, London W.1

GLASGOW NEW YORK TORONTO MELBOURNE WELLINGTON
CAPE TOWN SALISBURY IBADAN NAIROBI LUSAKA ADDIS ABABA
BOMBAY CALCUTTA MADRAS KARACHI LAHORE DACCA
KUALA LUMPUR HONG KONG

First issued in this edition 1964
Reprinted 1965

PRINTED IN GREAT BRITAIN BY THE CAMELOT PRESS LTD.
LONDON AND SOUTHAMPTON

PRINCIPLES OF LANGUAGE-STUDY

Editor's Preface

Harold E. Palmer was one of the leading specialists in the theory and practice of teaching English as a foreign language in the first half of the present century, so it is eminently fitting that one of his works should be included in the first group of books to be published in this series. His first important book on method, *The Scientific Study and Teaching of Languages*, appeared in 1917 and was immediately recognized as a new landmark in the literature of the subject. Sweet, Jespersen, and others had outlined the fundamental basis for the practical study of languages, and now Palmer took their ideas a stage further, enlarging on the general principles they had laid down and working out specimen programmes in considerable detail.

Shortly after the end of the First World War Palmer had a memorable meeting with an old friend, Charles Lemaire, a specialist in the teaching of French as a foreign language. Palmer, himself an enthusiast, was deeply impressed by Lemaire's fervour and by the similarity of their views. *The Principles of Language-Study* was written as a direct result of their conversation. In fact he began to write it the same day. The book is, not surprisingly, dedicated to Lemaire.

Palmer justifies the writing of a second book on the method of studying and teaching languages so soon after the appearance of the first by pointing out that the two differ both in content and in presentation. The first book contained a study of the nature of language and an analysis of the problems of teaching languages to different groups of students for different purposes, together with a lengthy discussion of the role of the teacher. Many of the suggestions put forward in the book were tentative and deliberately vague; and free use was made of 'scientific' or technical terms.

The Principles of Language-Study, on the other hand, presupposes the acceptance by the reader of Palmer's previous statements about the nature of language and deals, in less technical language, with 'the essential principles which must be observed by those who wish to teach—or learn—successfully.' It is pre-eminently a *practical* book.

Much more is known now about the psychology of language-learning than was available to Palmer in 1921, and some of his affirmations are at variance with more recent findings. We may not be able to accept his distinction between 'conscious' and 'unconscious' learning, but we cannot quarrel with his main thesis: that the intellectual understanding of how a language works is one thing, and the development of skill in using it is another. If we take Palmer's term 'unconscious assimilation' to refer at times to the *goal* (his 'automatism') rather than to the process of learning, we shall find little to object to in his analysis. And this little is vastly outweighed by the obvious relevance of most of the principles and procedures he advocates.

Palmer once asked me if I had any idea for what aspect of his work he would be remembered. Was there, he wondered, any particular contribution he had made that would be specially valued? It was not easy to answer his question. The suggestion that his writings on method constituted his most valuable work did not satisfy him, in view of his wider linguistic interests; but from the point of view of the language teacher, it is probably true. Palmer wondered, too, wherein lay his most original contribution within the general field of methodology. He himself was reluctant to put a name to his 'method', shying away from the term 'eclectic' (see Chapter 15) because of its unsatisfactory associations; but the term is often used now to refer to the kind of approach he advocated. It has largely shed the meaning that Palmer feared might become attached to it, and is interpreted as implying (in his words) 'the deliberate choice of all things which are good, a judicious and reasoned selection of all those diverse factors the sum of which may constitute a complete and homogeneous system.'

R. MACKIN

Contents

CHAPTER 1

Our spontaneous capacities for acquiring Speech

What do we do in order to become skilful in the exercise of an art? If we wish to become proficient in performing an unlimited series of complicated acts, what course do we adopt in order to obtain such proficiency? The first answer which suggests itself is to the effect that such skill or proficiency is acquired by a process called *study* or *learning*. We learn to do it; we *study* the art; we follow a course and all that the course implies; we attend lectures, we take lessons, we read the textbook containing the principles (rudimentary or otherwise) which embody the precepts relating to that art, we perform exercises; in short, we become *students*. Very well; let us accept the answer for what it is worth and proceed to formulate a series of supplementary questions: What are the qualities which mark the successful student? What sort of people are likely to study with success? Of what people can we predict failure or incapacity for making progress? Most people will answer: The student must possess intelligence, assiduity, and perseverance; if at the same time he should be 'gifted', his progress will be much greater than the progress of one who possesses no 'natural talents' for learning the art in question.

This answer, on the face of it, seems a reasonable one and a right one; it gives us the impression of being in accordance with the traditions and maxims of the pedagogic world, and with our experience, either as teachers or as learners. We think of our efforts (successful or unsuccessful) to learn shorthand, piano-playing, violin-playing, singing, chess, typewriting, dancing, drawing, painting, modelling, carpentering, and a host of similar subjects; we remember the intensive acts of analysis and synthesis, the efforts of attention, the strain of comprehending, the striving to retain; we remember the hours of solid labour, the exercises, the drills, the spade-work; we consider the period of time covered by these continuous efforts, and we realize the cost at which we have acquired our present proficiency.

And yet there exists an art, we are told, in which every one of us has become proficient, an art in which every man, woman, and child throughout the world is a skilful adept, an art which has been acquired without any process resembling study, without lectures or lessons or textbooks or theory, without the exercise of our powers of conscious or critical reflection, or analysis, or synthesis, or generalization, without the giving of our conscious attention, without deliberate effort or striving.

This art, we are told, requires no intelligence on the part of the one who is learning it; on the contrary, the least intelligent often prove to be among the most successful adepts, notably very young children, idiots, or barbarians of the lowest scale.

This statement seems so strange on the face of it, so paradoxical and so contrary to our preconceived notions concerning the acquiring of knowledge, that we immediately suspect some 'catch'; we are inclined to treat as a joker the one who has so gravely made the statement. The 'art' in question is probably something of an absurdly rudimentary character, something of such a simple nature that it neither admits of analysis or synthesis nor requires any form of logical or coordinated thought. But no, the art in question is one involving at least three distinct sciences, each of which is so complex and so vast that the learned world has not yet succeeded in unravelling it or in sounding its depths.

Convinced by now that we are the object of some form of ingenious witticism, we ask: What, then, is this strange art in which the dunce excels, this art which requires of its adepts neither brains, industry, nor patience?

The answer is: *The art of using the spoken and everyday form of any given language.* Show me the child of three years of age, the madman, or the savage, who is not an expert at it!

Let us make sure that we have understood this answer, in order that we may not misinterpret it, in order that we may not read into it a meaning which is not there. In the first place, there is no question here of *reading* or *writing* the language, but of *understanding what is said*, and of *expressing what we wish to say by speaking*; and the art in question has nothing to do with alphabets, with letters, with spelling, with calligraphy, which are artificial developments deliberately invented by man. Nor is there any question of *literary composition* in prose or poetry; we are not dealing with any aesthetic form, but merely with the 'everyday' form, the colloquial form, the sort of speech we use on ordinary occasions in order to express our usual thoughts. Let there be no mistake on this point: the higher forms of language, the artistic developments, eloquence or literature, may interest us, may interest us intensely, but the particular art of which we are now speaking is far removed from these heights; we are considering language as manifested by the normal colloquial form as used by the average speaker in ordinary circumstances.

Now there is no doubt whatever that proficiency in this particular sort of human activity is possessed by every human being who is not congenitally deaf or dumb; we are all able to say what we want to say, we are all able to understand what is said to us provided that the communication concerns things which are within the limits of our knowledge. We have acquired this proficiency not by a course of study as we understand the term in its ordinary use; we have not learnt it as a result of lectures or lessons; it has not come as a consequence of deliberate effort and concentration. Some of us, in exceptional circumstances, may have availed ourselves of our intelligence; but in general our intelligence, our reasoning powers, our capacities for deduction, for analysis and synthesis, have counted for nothing in the process.

Might we not then call it a 'gift'? Did we not mention specifically that those who have a gift for a particular art can to a certain extent dispense with the qualities of intelligence, assiduity, perseverance? There is no objection against using the term 'gift', provided that it is clear to our minds that everybody possesses the gift in question. Usually, however, we understand by 'gift' something 'given' to certain individuals only; consequently we are not in the habit of speaking about the gift of sight, of hearing, or of locomotion. It would be safer to avoid the term and to speak rather of our natural, spontaneous, and universal *capacity* for using spoken language.

But are we right as to our facts? Is it true that we acquire speech by some capacity other than our intelligence, our reasoning powers? Let our answer be based on objective and easily proven evidence. A child of two or three years of age can use the spoken language appropriate to his age, but what does that child know of reasoning? And what is its standard of intelligence? Not enough to cause it to realize or understand that two and two make four. And yet that child observes with a marvellous degree of accuracy most of the complicated law governing his mother tongue. And the savage. By definition he is unintelligent, he has never learnt to think logically, he has no power of abstraction, he is probably unaware that such a thing as language exists; but he will faithfully observe to the finest details the complexities (phonetic, grammatical, and semantic) of his 'savage' language. He will use the right vowel or tone in the right place; he will not confuse any of the dozen or so genders with which his language is endowed; a 'savage' language (with an accidence so rich that Latin is by comparison a language of simple structure) will to him be an instrument on which he plays in the manner of an artist, a master: and we are speaking of a savage, mark you, whose intelligence is of so low an order that for him that which is not concrete has no existence!

In English we have a tone-system so complicated that no one

has so far discovered its laws, but little English children observe each nicety of tone with marvellous precision; a learned specialist in 'tonetics' (or whatever the science of tones will come to be called) may make an error, but the little child will not. The grammatical system of the Bantu languages depends largely on fine shades of intonation; the dropping of the voice a semitone at certain points in the sentence, for instance, is an essential feature of their syntax, while the highly complex system of tone-mutation serves as a basis of their conjugation and declension; but no Bechuana or Matabele native, illiterate as he may be, will ever commit the slightest error in the use of his tones.

When, therefore, we find that a person has become expert in a difficult and complex subject, the theory of which has not yet been worked out, nor yet been discovered, it is manifest that his expertness has been acquired otherwise than by the study of the theory.

Let us furthermore examine what passes in our mind when we are speaking our own language, and endeavour to ascertain whether we form our sentences in unconscious obedience to some rules unknown to us, or whether we are consciously applying rules we have learnt. Do you say *I go always there* or *I always go there*? You certainly use the latter form. Why? Have you ever been told that a certain class of adverbs (among them the word *always*) is placed before and not after the verb? Have you been told that there are twenty-three exceptions to the rule, and have you ever learnt these exceptions? It is most probable that you have never had your attention called to the rule or to its exceptions. You put *always* in front of all verbs except the twenty-three exceptional verb-forms for the very reason for which the African native puts the right tone on the right syllable in the right case. In what cases do you replace the word *far* by the expression *a long way*? What are the precise laws governing the respective uses of *went* and *did go*? Which are the English 'postpositions', if any? In what cases do we use

5

nouns unpreceded by any article or other determinative word? What is the exact difference between *had you* and *did you have*? These are a few odd examples chosen at random out of the thousands of items the sum of which constitutes the theory of the structure of the English colloquial language. Most of them are not contained in any manual of English grammar nor ever taught as a school subject.

We are forced to conclude that we have become proficient in the use of our mother tongue by some process other than that of learning by dint of conscious efforts of reasoning and synthesis.

While granting the above conclusion and recognizing its validity, some may object that the process of unconscious assimilation is *not* sufficient to ensure skill and proficiency in the use of the language. This objection may be supported by proofs to the effect that the English of young children (not to mention adults) is frequently 'incorrect' or 'ungrammatical'. Can this process of nature be said to have succeeded when it produces such results as 'Any bloke what don't do it proper didn't ought to come'? Certainly the process has succeeded; most certainly the natural forces have operated with perfect success! The only trouble is that users of such sentences have succeeded in learning a dialect which most of us agree to consider a deplorable one; this dialect is to our ears an ugly and a repelling one, but in itself it is probably no easier to learn than the educated colloquial. An educated person to whom this dialect is foreign would probably have to pass a long period of study should he wish, for any particular purpose, to become expert in its use. It is quite a fallacy to suppose that a debased or vulgar form of speech is of easier acquisition than the more elevated forms. The language, dialect, patois, or form of speech taught by nature to the child (or adult) is that form which he hears spoken by those about him during the period of acquisition, be it the stilted speech of the pedant or the jargon of the slums.

Let us accept the thesis as so far proven; let us agree that this spontaneous capacity exists, that every child does become expert in this art, and that his expertness has been gained by the exercise of some powers other than those of conscious reflection or reasoning. But does not this relate solely to the acquisition of one's mother tongue? In the definition of the art in question the term 'any given language' was used. Do we conclude that this given language is the *first* language, or are we assuming that the same process holds good for any *foreign* or *subsequently learnt* language?

The question is a legitimate one; we may well ask ourselves whether the forces which were operative in the case of our first language are available for the acquisition of a second, third, or fourth language. Let us, as before, go to the actual facts and collect objective evidence on the point. What evidence is afforded by bilingual children, that is to say, by children who have learnt two languages simultaneously, children of mixed parentage, children whose care has been entrusted to foreign nurses, children who live abroad with their parents? In nearly all the cases of which we have any record it would appear that the two languages have been acquired simultaneously without mutual detriment; there has been practically no confusion between the two, and the one has had little or no influence on the other. Both have been acquired by the natural language-teaching forces which are at present engaging our attention.

The next evidence will consist of the testimony afforded by children who started their second language after the first had already been acquired as a going concern. We find almost invariably that the second language is picked up with the same facility and accuracy as the first. Thousands of Belgian refugee children returned to their country in possession of an English speech hardly to be distinguished from the speech of English children of their own age. Their first language had interfered in no way with their power of acquiring the second. There were, however, exceptions; in some instances the possession of the first language did interfere with the proper acquiring of the

7

second. What was the determining factor? To what was due this differentiation? We find that in most cases the child was of a riper age, he had arrived at the age of intelligence, and had been forced to use his rudimentary intelligence as a means towards learning English. He was old enough and clever enough to receive eye-impressions side by side with ear-impressions. He was old enough to pay attention, he was intelligent enough to concentrate, he was skilful enough to analyse and to compare the second language with his first, he was able to translate. These things had a harmful influence on his work; they interfered with the processes by which nature causes us to assimilate and to remember, and the quality of his English suffered; it was to a certain extent 'foreigner's' English, whereas his younger brothers spoke 'English' English.

And what happens in the case of the adult, of one who starts his second language from fifteen to twenty years after he has acquired the first? The same thing generally happens as in the last instance quoted, but in a more marked degree. The same interference takes place; the use of the eyes inhibits the use of the ears; the utilization of his conscious and focused attention militates against the proper functioning of the natural capacities of assimilation. Moreover, he is encouraged and trained to use the non-natural methods, he is directed by his teacher to pay attention to everything, to use his eyes, to memorize spellings (generally non-phonetic); his books show him how to analyse, they provide him with exercises calculated to make him concentrate on the detail, and in so doing to miss the synthetic whole. Examine the adult who is supposed to have 'learnt' a foreign language; in the majority of cases you will find that his speech is pidgin-speech, and that his sounds are wrong and wrongly distributed, that his inflexions are inaccurate, that his sentences are constructed on the model of his native language, that he uses foreign words in a way unknown to the native users of these same words. Inquire in each case how the person acquired his knowledge, and you will find that he acquired it by dint of exercising his capacities for study.

And the minority? We find a minority (alas, a small minority!) who have come to possess the foreign language as if it were their first. Their sounds are right, the distribution is right, the inflexions are accurate, their sentences are constructed on the model of those used by the native speakers, they use foreign words as the natives themselves use them, they are as accurate and as fluent in the foreign language as in their own. They do not interrupt the speaker of the language with requests to speak more slowly, to speak more distinctly, to spell or to write the words; in short, they use the second language as they use their first. Inquire in each case how the person acquired his knowledge, and you will find that he acquired it by methods making no call on his capacities for reasoning, for concentrating, for analysing, or for theorizing. Instead of selecting and adapting previously acquired habits connected with his first language, he was able to form new habits.

To sum up our inquiry, we find that there are people who have been able to use their spontaneous capacities of assimilation in order to acquire a second or a third language; we find that young children nearly always do so, that certain adults sometimes do so.

But we must make quite sure of our ground before proceeding farther. We must ascertain definitely whether all adults possess what we are calling this spontaneous capacity for assimilation, or whether this is a 'gift' in the usual acceptation of the term, that is, whether it is a capacity given to some but withheld by nature from others. Some maintain that from the age of reason onwards none but the gifted possess the capacity in question, and that those who do not possess it are bound to use what we shall call the *studial* processes. Others, on the contrary, maintain that all possess the capacity either in an active or in a latent state, that most adults deliberately but innocently inhibit their power, or that, unaware that these powers exist, they fail to take the necessary steps to awaken them from their latent into their active state.

Which of these two is the correct view?

Let us endeavour to answer this all-important question by examining those who undoubtedly do possess this 'gift' or natural capacity. We first inquire whether they were encouraged or disposed to resist the temptation to receive their impressions through the eyes, to resist the temptation to rely on spellings, whether they did consent to use their ears as the receptive medium. In each case we learn that they were so disposed; they did resist the temptation towards eye-work and did allow the ears to perform the work for which they were intended.

We next inquire whether the conditions were such as prohibited them from focusing their consciousness, from paying an exaggerated attention to detail, from submitting the language-matter to a form of analysis, from comparing each foreign word or form with some word or form of their native language. In each case we are informed that such *were* the conditions.

Our next inquiry is directed towards ascertaining whether, in the earlier stages, the conditions afforded them full and constant opportunities of hearing the language used, *without being under the necessity of speaking it themselves*. In each instance we are informed that those were precisely the conditions.

This is almost conclusive; we have ascertained that each successful acquirer of the foreign language was working precisely under the conditions enjoyed by the young child (and we remember that the young child is invariably a successful acquirer of foreign languages). It is, however, not conclusive enough; we have yet to inquire under what conditions the other type of adult (the supposedly non-gifted one) had been working. We ask the same three sets of questions, and in answer we learn:

(*a*) That he was encouraged by his teachers to learn by the medium of his eyes, to base his knowledge on spellings (generally non-phonetic), and in so doing to inhibit his ears from fulfilling their natural function.

(*b*) That he generally focused his consciousness, that he paid attention to detail, that he studied rules and practised analysis, that he constantly established comparisons between the foreign word and the nearest native equivalent.

(*c*) That conditions were such that he had few or no opportunities of hearing the language used, while he was obliged to use the language himself, to forge out sentences as best he might, neglectful of accuracy and heedless of their conformity or non-conformity with authentic models.

This is conclusive; there is no doubt about it now. Those who seemingly do not possess the spontaneous capacity for assimilating *foreign* languages are precisely those who were unwilling to avail themselves of it, or who were precluded from availing themselves of it. And by developing their studial powers they simply inhibited the spontaneous powers and effectively prevented them from working.

No reasonable doubt remains: we are all endowed by nature with certain capacities which enable each of us, without the exercise of our powers of study, to assimilate and to use the spoken form of any colloquial language, whether native or foreign. We may avail ourselves of these powers by training ourselves deliberately to utilize them, or, having more confidence in our studial efforts, or for some reason of special expediency, we may choose to leave our spontaneous capacities in their latent state and make no use of them. We cannot, however, afford to ignore them, and it would be foolish to deny their existence.

We shall see later what steps we must take if we wish to rouse those powers from their latent state, what we must do if we wish to enlist them and have them at our disposal for the purpose of learning or of teaching a foreign language.

CHAPTER 2

Our studial capacities and how to use them

We have seen that each of us possesses certain spontaneous capacities for learning how to use the spoken form of any language or variety of language. We have seen that these capacities may be either in a latent or an active state. We have seen that unless we enlist these powers in our service we are unlikely to make any real progress in language-study, either in point of quality or quantity. We shall see later by what means we may awaken our latent capacities and cause them to become active, and, incidentally, how we can exercise ourselves to make the fullest use of them.

But we also possess capacities other than these for assimilating and using a language. It is our purpose in the present chapter to see what these are, and to differentiate between them and those already described.

In the first place, let us note carefully that we have so far dealt with no other form of language than the normal spoken colloquial, that form which is used under normal conditions by the average educated native. We have not been considering any written form of language whatever, either colloquial or classical, nor have we given any attention to the more classical or literary form of speech whether spoken or written. We have, indeed, alluded to these aspects or varieties of language, but merely in order to state that they are beyond the range of any truly *spontaneous* capacities. Reading and writing are not spontaneous processes; they are even *unnatural* processes if we do not already possess the spoken form. Learning how to use classical or artificialized forms of language such as poetry or rhetoric is a more or less studial process, an unnatural process if we do not already possess the normal colloquial. For this, then, if not for other reasons, we must be prepared to adopt certain forms of work unknown to man in his natural state (as exemplified by the very young child); we shall allude to these as the '*studial* methods'.

What, then, are these studial methods? Roughly speaking, we may say that they comprise all those forms of work which require on the part of the student *conscious efforts of attention*; work in which he must think, reflect, or calculate; work necessitating the exercise of his reasoning powers, work which cannot be performed automatically; this constitutes conscious work, and all methods embodying conscious work become *ipso facto* studial methods.

Most work of analysis and synthesis is of this order; all that we do to break up a sentence into words, into syllables, into sounds; all that we do to piece together sounds, syllables, and words in order to form sentences is of this order. Whenever we are distinctly conscious of the words and constructions we are using, we are doing something unknown to nature. Whenever we come to understand a sentence by analysing it, or to utter a sentence by piecing together as we go on, we are working by processes of the studial order; they were not used when we were learning our mother tongue.

All those forms of work which we may include under the heading of 'conversion' are studial, and these are many and varied. Dictation consists in causing the pupil to convert the spoken into the written aspect of language, reading consists in causing him to do the reverse, most forms of translating consist in causing him to convert something from one language into another. We may also at times require our pupils to convert an affirmative sentence into a negative or an interrogative one, to convert a present tense into a past, a singular into a plural, passive into active, to convert a certain word-order into another.

All these things are of the studial order; sound they may be, necessary or essential they may be, but they are not spontaneous forms of work, for we have not by their aid learnt to use the spoken colloquial form of our mother tongue.

All methods which necessitate the use of the eye are studial methods; nature never meant us to learn spoken language by eye. We may therefore designate as studial all forms of reading, reading aloud or mental reading, reading from traditional orthographies or phonetic transcriptions, reading of isolated sounds or of connected passages. More especially of the studial order are those curious and complicated practices (common, alas! to so many students) of 'reading what we hear' or 'writing what we speak'. In the former case, we hear a sentence, we reduce it mentally to written characters, and read mentally what we see in our imagination; in the other case we write in our imagination what we wish to say, and read aloud what we are writing.

It follows that all methods which require us to use the hand are studial methods; nature knows no more of spellings and handwriting than she does of shorthand, typewriting, and type-setting; all these things are of comparatively recent origin, and all of them have been deliberately invented by man.

All methods which teach meanings by means of etymology are of the studial order; nature intended that each word should become attached to that for which it stands and not become associated with its ancestral etymon or modern cognates. The dictum of nature is that a word means what all speakers of the same language (or variety of language) mean it to mean.

Thus it would appear that nearly everything that the average person actually does when learning a foreign language comes under the heading of the studial processes. He learns rules in order to become proficient in analysis and synthesis; for the same purpose, he memorizes the exceptions to the rules. He becomes (or hopes to become) an expert in pulling words to pieces and in reconstructing them from roots and affixes, in sentence-making and sentence-breaking. He learns chiefly by eye, and expresses himself chiefly by the pen-grasping hand. Indeed, he becomes so proficient in converting the spoken into the written form that he cannot understand or retain the foreign words or sentences he learns until he has converted them into an imaginary written form which, in his imagination, he reads off word by word. Similarly, he finds himself only able to express himself by dint of reading aloud the sentences which he is constructing bit by bit by a complicated process of 'mental writing'. He aims at becoming (and often does become) expert in converting one language into another by a process (unknown to nature) called translating. His accuracy is gained by rapid conversions of words from one inflected form to another: nominatives into accusatives, singulars into plurals, infinitives into participles. He attaches great importance to etymology, and the time he might spend in associating words with their meanings is often devoted to working out the family tree of foreign words. He spends little time in finding out what meanings the natives attach to their words and forms, but much time in identifying the units of etymology and in tracing them from one language to another.

This does not necessarily imply that the student is always doing the wrong thing, nor that his methods are always bad ones; we merely observe that he uses (or is taught to use) all manner of studial methods at the expense of spontaneous ones, and that, in so doing, he develops his studial capacities of language-study at the expense of his spontaneous ones. The question whether the studial methods should be used at all and, if so, which should be used, forms the subject of the next chapter.

CHAPTER 3

Why we must use our studial capacities

We should not conclude that methods involving our powers of study are to be abandoned, and that nature alone is to be responsible for our linguistic education. On the contrary, we suggest that an extensive use be made of powers which are not possessed by the young child or the barbarian.

In the first place, nature will not teach us to read or to write, but merely to become proficient in the use of the *spoken* form of a given language. However valuable it may be to possess the spoken form, most of us wish to go beyond this; we wish eventually to be able to use some form of orthography. Some even desire to go beyond this and to learn to use shorthand or the typewriter, man-made inventions of a still more recent date. For we must remember that, after all, traditional orthography is not a whit more 'natural' than shorthand, and a good deal less 'natural' than phonetic transcription or reformed spelling.

To learn, however, the written form of a language before having learnt how to assimilate the spoken form is unnatural and contrary to all our linguistic instincts; it is comparable to learning how to cycle before having learnt to walk. At a certain stage, therefore, the learner will be taught how to recognize by eye what he has already assimilated by ear, and how to express with the pen what he has hitherto expressed by means of articulate sounds. In each case the process will be one of conversion, converting written characters into sounds or converting sounds into written characters. In both cases there will be articulation of some sort, for mental reading means mental articulation, and when we write we only write what we are repeating to ourselves mentally.

Neither of these forms of conversion is necessarily difficult. The processes, without being spontaneous in the true sense of the term, present at times certain analogies to truly spontaneous processes in that they are apparently performed without effort. Much depends, however, on the system of script; if the alphabet of the foreign language is almost identical with an alphabet we have already learnt to use, the difficulty will be less than in the case of a totally strange alphabet or syllabary. Japanese script, which contains a strange mixture of Chinese characters used both ideographically and phonetically, together with two different systems of native phonetic writing, presents difficulties unknown to the European student of European languages.

The artificial element in writing is particularly evident when we consider that many if not most orthographic systems are in contradiction to the spoken form of the languages they claim to represent. English spelling is an excellent case in point; its divergences from the actual language are so numerous and so great that we may be said to possess two distinct languages, the spoken and the written. To learn and to apply the arbitrary laws and conventions which serve to bridge the gap between the two requires capacities of observation and reasoning of a special order, essentially studial. For that reason we must make use of conversion devices of various kinds: dictation, reading aloud, transcription (or transliteration), and spelling drill. Many so-called 'difficulties of grammar' prove to be mere difficulties of spelling; the French conjugation and what remains of French declension are largely matters of spelling, often as baffling to the native French speaker as to the non-French student.

There are other reasons why studial methods must be adopted in a complete language-course. There exist forms of speech other than the form which is used normally in everyday conversation. There exist artificialized non-colloquial dialects, such as poetry, the language of emotion and oratory, the language of ceremony, the liturgical, and similar classical or archaic varieties. As we have already seen, nature teaches us only those living forms which are used by the people of our environment; for the others we must have recourse to studial methods. The everyday colloquial form is something we learn at home or in the street; the higher or more aesthetic forms are taught us at school or at college; we have to *study* them. The art of literary composition, the art of selecting and assembling deliberately and consciously those words which express our thoughts and emotions in the clearest and most appropriate manner, differs widely and essentially from the art of colloquy as exercised in our daily life. In order to become proficient in literary composition, we must acquire habits of concentration, we must be able to analyse, we must become expert in synthesis, we must learn to discriminate, we must develop our intelligence. The young child cannot do these things, nor can the savage or the idiot.

There is another reason why we cannot leave everything to nature: most language-courses must necessarily be *corrective courses*. The teacher generally finds among his adult students a large number who have already acquired certain notions of the language; they may have spent one or more years working at school-French, school-English, or whatever the language may be; they may have spent some time in the country where it is spoken, or they may have studied privately. In most of these cases it is practically certain that the student will have formed bad linguistic habits; his pronunciation will be deplorable, his command of the inflected forms will be deficient, his syntax will be faulty, and his semantic system will be that of his native tongue. In other terms, he has acquired a pidgin form of the language, such as Anglo-French or Franco-English, unnatural dialects unknown to native speakers; he may have become accustomed to using this form of language, even to using it automatically. Nor is that all; not only is his language-material faulty (to say the least of it), but his manner of study will probably have impaired very seriously his capacities for any sound form of assimilation. He has not been trained to observe nor to imitate nor to construct sentences by analogy; he has so trained himself to hearing what he expects to hear and what he thinks he hears that he has no notion of what he actually does hear; in short, he has generally learnt wrong material in wrong ways.

The only suitable course for such a student would be a corrective course, a course which would aim at replacing his faulty material by sound material and at replacing his former methods of study by sound methods. One by one his unsound acquisitions must be replaced by sound ones; we must teach him a new language. Now this cannot be done by means of spontaneous methods alone; unconsciousness will not undo the work consciousness has done; the natural powers which enable us to assimilate normal speech will rarely, if ever, turn bad habits into good ones or convert pidgin-speech into normal speech. What has been done consciously must be undone consciously. The student must be shown specifically in what respects his speech differs from that used by natives, and he must deliberately set to work to correct it item by item; we must explain things to him; we must provide him with charts, diagrams, and exercises; we must put him through courses of drill-work, and all these things will require his careful and even concentrated attention. We must also teach him how to correct his faulty methods of assimilating; we must explain to him why they are faulty and convince him that, however natural and easy they may seem to him, they are only of utility to the learner of pidgin-speech. We must teach him how to utilize the sound processes (both spontaneous and studial); he will not like to do so, he will constantly tend to revert to the processes to which he has become accustomed; we must react and cause him to react against his vicious tendencies. After a time, if

B

fortunate, we may succeed in eradicating most of the faulty matter and in initiating the right habits of assimilation. From that point onwards the course will not be a corrective one but a normal one.

Do these considerations apply only to one who has already studied the language faultily, to the use of pidgin-speech? Are we to take it that the raw beginner is exempt from unnatural or vicious habits? Unfortunately this is not the case: more often than not, the student (even the student unspoiled by previous defective work) will tend to let his first language influence his second. If he is English, he will tend to insinuate English sounds, English forms, and English thoughts into the new language, which will therefore tend to become pidginized. This tendency will be greater with some than with others; much depends on the attitude of the student towards the language he is about to learn; he may already have studied other foreign languages, and in doing so may have acquired the wrong attitude towards foreign languages in general. If he considers them as branches of study similar to mathematics, history, or geography; or if he considers them essentially as orthographic systems of which the phonetic form is an unimportant detail, he will already have become one for whom a corrective course is necessary. We shall have to remove his prejudices and to modify his point of view; a certain amount of preliminary work will have to be done in order that he may see languages as they really are, in order that he may see the nature of the task before him. This preliminary work will be of the studial order, but will be succeeded at the right moment by the more normal and more spontaneous methods. On the other hand, many students start with no preconceived ideas whatever; children, the less intelligent adults, and those who have been unspoiled by the traditional classical fallacies will slip easily and naturally into the right attitude. They will recognize the necessity for learning new sounds and combinations, for assimilating foreign material without at each instant comparing it with the material of the mother-tongue; for retaining by the auditory memory strings of words and sentences, for reproducing orally what they hear, and for forming the right semantic associations. Such students will be immune or nearly so from the vicious tendencies which so characterize the average language-learner; they will merely have to be put on their guard at certain critical moments; we shall at such moments observe certain reasonable precautions in order that bad habits may not be acquired.

A fourth reason why we must not neglect the studial methods may be mentioned here. Many set out not so much to acquire the capacity for using the language as to learn its structure and peculiarities, just as a mechanic may wish to become acquainted with a machine without having the intention of ever using it. Phoneticians, grammarians, and philologists must in the ordinary course of their work become familiar with the characteristic features of many languages or dialects. For this purpose it is by no means necessary that they should acquire the capacity for unders nding, speaking, reading, or writing the languages which interest them.

In such cases the spontaneous methods would obviously be out of place; no call need be made or should be made on the students' natural powers of language-assimilating. They would proceed by way of analysis and synthesis, and instead of retaining the actual language-material itself would retain merely the laws which govern the functioning of the language.

We might place in this category of students those whose subsequent intention is to teach the language to others. It may not be necessary for the language-*learner* to know much about the theory of phonetics, but the language-*teacher* must possess a considerable knowledge of phonetic theory both general and as applied to the particular language in which he is an instructor. The learner need know little about the sciences dealing with inflexions, sentence-construction, or meanings; but the teacher must know a good deal about these things in order that he may foresee the special difficulties which his pupils will encounter, and devise the necessary exercises to overcome them. The technical side of language will therefore be of importance to all who are or who intend to become teachers, and such knowledge, like any other technical knowledge, is acquired by methods unrelated to our spontaneous capacities for assimilating normal colloquial speech.

The four series of considerations set forth above are sufficient to show that it would be either unwise or impossible to proceed by the sole aid of nature or by the reconstitution of natural conditions. Language-study is such a complex thing, with so many aspects, and it requires to be looked at from so many points of view, that we must enlist *all* our capacities when striving to obtain the mastery we desire; we must not neglect our spontaneous powers, nor should we despise our intellectual powers; both are of service to us, both have their place in a well-conceived programme of study, each will to a certain extent balance the other and be complementary to it. An excess on either side may be prejudicial to the student, and one of the more important problems before the speech-psychologist is to determine in what circumstances and on what occasions each should be used. More will be said on this particular phase of the subject in Chapter 15 ('The Multiple Line of Approach').

CHAPTER 4

The student and his aim

What is the best method of language-study? This fundamental question is one which is continually asked by all those who are seriously engaged in teaching or in learning a foreign language. We say 'seriously' and lay stress on the word, for among teachers and students there are many, unfortunately, who are not disposed to take their work seriously, who see no necessity for any earnest consideration of the ways and means to be adopted. They are content to teach as they themselves have been taught, or to learn as others have learnt before them, without inquiring whether the plan or the programme is a sound one, without even inquiring whether the method is one which is likely to produce any good results whatever. But the serious teacher or student, who wishes to perform efficient work, must of necessity ask himself whether the path he has chosen is one which will lead anywhere near the desired end or ends. He may experiment with various methods and try a number of different systems in order to ascertain which of these secures the best results, and after many such trials he may either hit upon what seems to be an ideal type of work and stick to it, or, dissatisfied with everything he has tried, he may once again seek counsel and ask once more the old and hackneyed question: What is the best method of language-study?

The first answer which suggests itself is: 'The best method is that which adopts the best means to the required end,' and indeed this is perhaps the only concise answer which can be furnished off-hand. But the answer is not satisfactory; it is too general, and so true that it ranks as a truism; it is resented as being a facetious manner of shelving the question. The inquirer has every right to return to the charge and to put the supplementary question: 'What is the method which adopts the best means to the required end?'

In the present book we shall endeavour to find the best answer or the best series of answers to this most legitimate question. In doing so we shall set forth, with as much precision as is consistent with the claims of conciseness, the conclusions arrived at by those who have specialized in the subject and have obtained positive evidence bearing on it.

Fundamental as the question appears, there is yet a previous question of which we must dispose before going further, for we cannot determine 'what is the best method adopting the best means towards the required end' until we know more precisely what *is* the required end.

For there are many possible ends, and many categories of students, each with a particular aim before him.

Many desire a knowledge of the written language only; they wish to be able to read and write, not to understand the spoken language nor to speak. Some may limit their attainment to a capacity for reading the language; they wish to have direct access to technical or other books. Others conceivably may wish solely to become able to write letters in the language. Many are only concerned with spoken language; they wish to be able to speak and to understand what they hear. Some wish to possess an 'understanding' knowledge only, while others are content merely to make themselves understood.

The student may limit his requirements to a very superficial knowledge of some pidgin form of the language, and will be perfectly happy if he just succeeds in making himself understood by using some atrocious caricature of the language which he is supposed to be learning. Or he may be more ambitious and set out in earnest to become master of the living language just as it is spoken and written by the natives themselves. The phonetician will wish to attain absolute perfection in the pronunciation of the language; the etymologist will concentrate on the historical aspect; the philologist will not be happy unless he is comparing the structure with that of cognate languages; the grammarian will specialize in grammar, and the lexicologist or semantician will study the meanings.

The clerk or merchant will specialize in the commercial language and learn how to draw up bills of lading or to conduct business correspondence. The hotel-keeper or waiter will concentrate on hotel colloquial, as also will the tourist or tripper. The *littérateur* will aim straight at the literature and disdain any of the non-aesthetic aspects or branches. Every calling or profession will seek its own particular line, and for each there will be a particular aim.

Many students have as their sole aim the passing of a given examination. Whether they come to know the language or not is a matter of comparative indifference to them; their business is to obtain as many marks as possible with the least amount of effort, and what does not lead directly to this aim is not of interest. It is the duty of many or most teachers to coach or to cram their pupils in order that satisfactory examination results may be obtained; they cannot afford to do anything else, nor have they any desire to do so. If the examination includes questions on phonetic theory, the pupil will be crammed with phonetic theory; if it includes a test in conversation, the pupil will be crammed with conversational tags; if it requires the capacity of translating, the pupil will duly be coached in the art of translating; if it requires a knowledge of a given text or series of texts, these will be the subject of study. If the pupil or his teacher knows something of the particular examiner, special efforts will be made to please that particular examiner. But this has little or nothing to do with the serious study of languages.

Some people are professional translators or interpreters; it is their business to render a faithful account of a speech or a sentence uttered in another language or to interpret the thoughts of some foreign writer. This work requires very special qualifications and necessitates a very special study, so much so that those who are perfectly bilingual experience a great difficulty every time that they are called upon to render a faithful translation of any document or a faithful interpretation of any oral communication. The task of the translator is quite distinct from that of the ordinary student of language, and is to be dealt with as such. Generally speaking, however, the language-learner will have comparatively little to do with the profession of interpreter or translator, and even in the exceptional cases he will do well to leave this particular branch until he has attained a certain proficiency in using the foreign language independently of any other. We have already alluded to the special requirements of the technician; we have seen that some require a knowledge of the structure or of certain aspects of one or more languages.

Such people, having entirely different aims, require entirely different methods; they must be furnished with everything that will facilitate their work of analysis or synthesis, and we may omit from their programme everything which does not lead directly towards the limited and special end they have in view.

Yet another factor is present and must be considered before we can draw up any definite programme of study. Are we giving a three months' course or a three years' course? If we are to obtain concrete and definite results in a limited space of time, our course must necessarily be an intensive one; we shall have to make a generous use of studial methods; we shall not be able to afford anything like an adequate period of preparation; we shall be forced to take short cuts and we shall reluctantly be compelled to sacrifice a certain measure of soundness to the requirements of speed. If, however, at the end of the short course to which circumstances limit our student's opportunity, he has a chance to continue his studies by himself or to reside in the country where the language is spoken, we may devote the whole of our time to preparatory work. We may give him an intensive course of ear-training, articulation, or fluency exercises, cause him to memorize a certain number of key-sentences, and drill him into good habits of language-study. If we adopted this plan we should be laying the foundations upon which the student would build later by his own initiative, but the drawback would be that the student would have made but small progress in the actual process of assimilating vocabulary; he would be well prepared, but would have little to show as a result of his two or three months' work.

If, on the other hand, we know that we have a clear period of two or more years before us, our task will be much easier. Instead of proceeding at a breathless rate to produce immediate concrete results, we may go to work in a more leisurely and more natural way. We may sow, and be assured that the harvest will be reaped in due time; the natural powers of language-study work surely but not rapidly; nature takes her time but yields a generous interest. With a long period in front of us, we may afford adequate intervals for 'incubation'; it will not be necessary for us to accelerate the normal process of assimilation, but merely to let it develop in a gradual but ever-increasing and cumulative ratio. At the end of, let us say, the first year, our student will easily outstrip those whose initial progress seemed more satisfactory.

Evidently it will not be possible to draw up a programme of study which will be suitable for all the diverse requirements we have set forth. Nor will it be possible for every teacher to consider the individual requirements of each one of his pupils. We cannot have a specially printed course, nor even a manuscript one, for every student; but in the case of private lessons or of self-instruction we may certainly give a large amount of consideration to individual needs. The bad pronouncer will concentrate on phonetic work, the bad speller on orthographic work, the bad listener on devices leading towards immediate comprehension; the clerk will work with texts of a commercial nature, the tourist will specialize on hotel colloquial, etc. No student will ever be expected to work with one book only;

each will gradually acquire a miniature library, and this library need not be the same for everybody.

In the case of collective courses and class teaching, individual requirements will be less observed, but in drawing up the programme the teacher will aim at the average result desired by or considered desirable for the average member of the class. As we shall see later, it is quite feasible to design lessons suitable for a class containing pupils of different capacities; we can arrange that some shall take an active part while others are assimilating more or less passively.

We see, in short, that when starting a new course under new conditions the teacher must draw up a programme. This programme will be divided into so many periods or stages, and for each period certain forms of work will be specified, these being designed to lead in the most efficient way to whatever the aim may happen to be. Without such a programme the teacher will never know exactly where his class stands, the work will be too much of a hand-to-mouth nature, and there will be loose ends. This programme may of course be more or less experimental or tentative; it may be modified in accordance with the teacher's experience and with the results he has so far obtained. The idea of a hard-and-fast programme does not commend itself; it should, on the contrary, be more or less elastic in order that it may be expanded or contracted according to circumstances. Anything in the nature of a 'patent method' (guaranteed to work within so many lessons) suggests quackery. Our programme should be something other than a rigid procedure based on any one particular principle, however logical that principle may seem to be. There are many logical principles, and we must strive to incorporate all of them into whatever programme we design. We shall treat of these in the next chapters.

CHAPTER 5

The supreme importance of the elementary stage

Before examining and reviewing the principles of language-study, it will be well for us to note one important point. The reader ere long may protest that we pay no attention to anything except beginner's work, that we examine no evidence bearing on the more advanced stages, that we give no advice nor offer any suggestions concerning the work of the second and subsequent years. 'We are not interested in elementary work,' some may say; 'what we require is a series of counsels as to how to conduct the subsequent (and more difficult) work.'

And yet we shall have little to say concerning the more advanced course; on the contrary, we shall constantly lay stress and insist on the supreme importance of the elementary stage.

It is the first lessons that count; it is the early lessons which are going to determine the eventual success or failure of the course. As the bending of the twig determines the form of the tree, as on the foundations depends the stability of the building, so also will the elementary training of the student determine his subsequent success or failure.

It is during the first stage that we can secure habits of accuracy, that we can train the student to use his ears, that we can develop his capacities of natural and rapid assimilation, that we can foster his powers of observation. Good habits are easily formed (as also are bad habits); at the outset of his studies the learner, whoever he may be, educated or illiterate, child or adult, enjoys the advantage of a plastic mind; it can be shaped according to our will; we can train it to form good and sound habits of language-study. At no other period shall we find such plasticity. Difficult, almost impossible, is the task of undoing what has already been done, of removing faulty habits of perception and of replacing them by sound ones. The student who has passed through an unsound elementary course finds his road to progress barred; the twig has been badly bent, the foundations have been badly laid. All we can then do is to endeavour by means of a corrective course to undo the mischief which has been done, and a thankless task it is. No amount of advanced work can fully compensate or make good the harm which has been wrought by the untrained or unwise teacher. It is too late. Certain habits have been formed, and we all realize what it means to eradicate a bad habit and to replace it by a good one.

What are some of these bad habits? What are the most characteristic vicious tendencies which have been encouraged by an unsound elementary stage? Some of these are positive, others are negative. In some cases the student has acquired bad habits; in others he has neglected to acquire good ones; often the two kinds are complementary to each other. We find, for instance, that he has neglected to train his ears, he has not been shown what to observe nor how to observe. The consequence is that he is unaware of the existence of certain foreign sounds, and invariably replaces them by absurd or impossible imitations based on the sounds of his mother tongue. Instead of French *é* he will use English *ay*; instead of French *on* he will use English *ong*; a trilled *r* will be replaced by an English fricative *r* or by no *r* at all.

Lack of ear-training will cause him to insert imaginary sounds where there are none. The French student will introduce an *r* (and a French *r* at that!) in words such as *course* or *farm*; he will insert a weak *e* (ə) in the *pl* of *people* or in the *bl* of *able*. He has never actually heard such sounds, but imagines that he has; his ears have not been trained to observe. He has formed the habit of replacing ear-impressions by eye-impressions; he believes what his eyes tell him, and his untrained ears cannot correct the tendency; he has become the dupe of unphonetic spellings.

The neglect of his powers of audition will cause him to rely absolutely on his powers of visualizing the written form. He will refuse to receive the language-matter by the auditory channel; he will declare with insistence that 'he cannot learn a word or a sentence until he has seen it written'; he will even decline to learn a word except in its traditional (and probably phonetically inaccurate) orthographic form.

If the elementary course has not provided for the development and use of the powers of unconscious assimilation, the student will attempt the hopeless task of passing the whole of the language-material through his limited channel of consciousness. He will seek to concentrate his attention on every simple unit of which the foreign language is composed, and hope thereby to retain every one, a feat of memory which we know to be impossible. He will therefore have formed the habit of deliberately avoiding that natural process which alone will enable him to make effective progress.

He will also have formed the 'isolating' habit, which consists in learning the individual elements of a group instead of learning the group as it stands. He will learn *chaise* instead of *la chaise*, *allé* instead of *suis allé* or *est allé*. In other terms, he will have formed the habit of word-learning and have neglected that of word-group-learning. Hence, instead of having at his disposal a number of useful compounds such as *Je ne le lui ai pas donné*, *Il n'y en a pas de ce côté-ci*, or *À cette époque-ci*, he will endeavour laboriously and generally unsuccessfully to build up by some synthetic process (probably that of literal translation) every word-group, phrase, or sentence in the language.

Had his elementary course included the systematic memorizing of word-groups, this would have become a habit; as it is, he has acquired the habit of not doing so.

Bad semantic habits may also have been formed. That is to say, the student may have trained himself (or even may have been trained) to consider that each foreign word corresponds precisely to some word in his own language. For him *prendre* is the exact equivalent of *to take*; *to get* is an untranslatable word, and many foreign words are meaningless!

If translation (not in itself a bad habit) has been carried to extremes, and if the habit of direct association has been neglected, the student will have formed the habit of translating mentally everything that he hears or reads, and this will be fatal to subsequent progress.

The principle of gradation may have been faultily applied in different ways. The teacher may have considered it his duty to over-articulate his words, to pause before each word, and to speak under the normal speed of five syllables per second. In this case the student will have formed the habit of understanding no form of speech other than this artificialized type. The capacity for understanding normal, rapid, and even under-articulated speech can only be developed by exercise in listening to such speech, and he will not have had this exercise.

The elementary programme may also have been drawn up in such a way as to preclude the study of irregular forms. If this has been the case, the student, unprepared for irregularities, will not know how to deal with them, and his rate of progress will be correspondingly diminished when they occur in more advanced work.

These are some of the bad habits, positive and negative, which will result from an unsound elementary course; these will be some of the fruits of early lessons which have not been based on the essential principles of language-teaching.

One of the functions of an elementary course is to enable the student to make use, even if only in a rudimentary way, of the language he is learning. It is therefore maintained by some that any form whatever of teaching which leads to such result may be considered as satisfactory. On these grounds it might be urged that, as pidgin-speech is better than no speech at all, we should at the outset aim at pidgin, and leave it to the more advanced stage to convert this type of speech into the normal variety as used by the natives.

But those who may hold this view forget that the elementary course has a second and more important function, viz. so to prepare the student that his subsequent rate of progress shall constantly increase.

The quantity of matter contained in even the everyday language is great—greater than most of us generally imagine. Not only are there thousands of words, but the majority of these consists of a group of allied forms, declensional, conjugational, and derivative. Very many words also stand for two, three, or more different meanings; moreover, the meaning of any word is influenced by the presence of other words in the same sentence. Were the beginner able to see in advance the full extent of the work that lies before him, he might abandon his task at the outset.

The work of assimilating this enormous mass of language-stuff will certainly never be accomplished on retail lines; it will not be done by mere efforts of analysis, synthesis, and eye-work. Unless the rate of progress increases continuously, unless the principle of gradation is observed strictly, there is no prospect of the student gaining the mastery of the language which is his aim.

It is the elementary stage, long or short, which will prepare the student for this increasing rate of progress, and an elementary course which has not so prepared the student cannot be said to have accomplished its purpose. It is during the elementary stage that we turn out the good or the bad worker. The function of the first lesson is not only to teach the language, but, more important still, *to teach the student how to learn.*

When we have instilled into him the habits of correct observation, of using his ears, of using his capacities for unconscious assimilation, of forming direct associations—in short, when we have taught him how to learn—the subsequent stages may safely be left to the student and to nature. Let us take care of the elementary stage, and the advanced stage will take care of itself.

33

CHAPTER 6

The principles of language-teaching

The art of method-writing (or of course-designing, which is not very different) is in its infancy; it has all the marks of the early or even primitive stage; it is in a state of slow evolution comparable to that which characterized the gradual perfecting of mechanical inventions and devices such as the typewriter, the bicycle, or the calculating machine. In the early stages of each of these (and many similar things) each model was more or less rudimentary and clumsy. A dozen different inventors working individually produced a dozen different machines; although all designed to accomplish the same work, the means adopted in each case differed fundamentally. In 1890 it was possible to distinguish even at a distance the make of any particular bicycle. At the present day we can still see great differences of structure between the different makes of typewriters and calculating machines. As time goes on, however, we notice a gradual convergence of types; one inventor profits by the work of others; in spite of the laws of patent, certain improvements are copied or adapted, individual defects are gradually eliminated and devices or dispositions which have proved their worth are adopted. The tendency is always towards the more perfect type, the more efficient apparatus; and the path towards perfection is marked by an ever-growing convergence of types. The ideal appears to be reached when there is practically no scope for further improvements; by that time the theoretical principles have been worked out and have become common property; what divergences do continue to exist are not concerned with essentials, they are merely variations of equal value. Were we to ask a hundred different bicycle-makers or boat-builders to design what they considered an ideal model, the hundred resultant models would be for all practical purposes identical.

Now, if we asked a hundred different language-teachers to design what each considered an ideal course or textbook, the result at the present day would certainly be a hundred different courses. They would differ in every conceivable way; most of them would differ from the others fundamentally. This would prove that the art in question is in a very early stage; it would prove that few or no fundamental principles are generally recognized. If, however, at some date in the distant future we were to make the same request, restricting our invitation to those who will have made a special study of the subject, to those who will have been striving towards perfection, we should probably find no great degree of diversity in the treatment; we should see the converging tendency at work, and should gather that the fundamental principles were beginning to stand out and to be respected. In the yet more distant future the answer to our request might take the form of a hundred manuscripts, all essentially the same, and differing only in non-essential details; we should then know that the fundamental principles had been established and had been accepted, but by that time none but experts in the subject will ever venture to carry out such highly technical work.

Much time will probably elapse before we arrive at this desirable state of things; much error will have to be eliminated and much experimental work will have to be accomplished. We shall have to ascertain exactly what does take place when we learn, and exactly what are the mental processes involved. We shall then have to grope about and feel our way, adopting and rejecting, modifying and adapting, improving and perfecting. We shall have to co-ordinate our efforts so that each may profit by the success or failure of fellow-workers; we shall have to experiment under all sorts of conditions, with all sorts of learners, and with all sorts of languages. There are distinct signs today that this kind of co-operation is coming about. We see, for instance, that the branch of language-study concerned with pronunciation is already far advanced in the experimental stage. For years past phoneticians have been busily engaged in research work; at first working apart, they are now coming together and pooling their efforts, each profiting by the discoveries of the others. A universal terminology is coming into existence; a universal phonetic alphabet is well on its way; the principles of phonetics and of phonetic transcription are developing rapidly, and the inevitable experts' quarrels are becoming more and more confined to matters of detail and to non-essentials. The remarkable advance in this comparatively new science is one of the most hopeful signs of progress, and a pledge of eventual perfection.

A similar advance in the sister sciences such as grammar and semantics is not yet apparent, but there are signs that ere long the many isolated workers in these domains will be able to do what the phoneticians did twenty or thirty years ago; they will enlist new workers, they will open up the field of research, they will draw up, first tentatively and then decisively, the broad principles on which the experimental and constructive work will repose, there will be co-ordinated and co-operative effort in many countries, and we shall witness the coming into existence of the general science of linguistics.

In the meantime, the subject is engaging the attention of psychologists. Strangely enough, the psychologists, whose function it is to ascertain how we learn, have not been consulted by writers of language-courses, and few of them have ever intervened in the matter. Each language-teacher has had to feel his way as best he could, proceeding empirically, dabbling in psychology, which meant that he did not always apply and often misinterpreted whatever principles of the subject he may have picked up. There are signs that speech-psychologists are about to co-ordinate their efforts with those of the phoneticians and with the experience of those who are actively engaged in making their language-teaching more efficient. We can point to more than one centre both in England and abroad where this co-operation is in its initial stage, and once this co-operation becomes an accomplished fact progress will be very rapid, and the progress will be sound. The work of Sweet, of Jespersen, and of de Saussure (to cite only three of our modern leaders) has already paved the way for the new and growing contingent of workers who are prepared to take up the threads and to weave them together in the fabric of the future.

What are the principles of language-study so far evolved? What are the fundamental axioms so far postulated? Do they give us the impression of soundness? Do they appear to us to be reasonable? Do they bear the aspect of finality? We shall judge. We shall endeavour to formulate the leading principles which have resulted from long periods of experimental work so far carried on by individual workers. The list will probably not be exhaustive, nor will the items be presented in that perfectly logical sequence which the future reserves for it. It will, however, seek to embody the largest number of important precepts under the smallest number of headings, in order that we may see in a concise form something which is still evolving and progressing towards further efficiency and simplicity. We purposely omit from the list certain minor principles and modes of application, nor can particular details connected with the study of particular languages be well included in the present work.

At the present day nine essential principles seem to stand out fairly clearly, and may provisionally be named as follows:

(1) Initial preparation.
(2) Habit-forming.
(3) Accuracy.
(4) Gradation.
(5) Proportion.
(6) Concreteness.

(7) Interest.
(8) Order of progression.
(9) Multiple line of approach.

We append a brief definition or broad description of these principles, and reserve for the following chapters a detailed explanation of each of them.

(1) *Initial Preparation.* During the initial stages of the course the teacher will, if necessary, endeavour by means of appropriate forms of exercise to awaken and to develop the student's natural or spontaneous capacities for language-study, in order that he may be adequately prepared for his subsequent work.

(2) *Habit-forming.* Language-study is essentially a habit-forming process; the teacher will therefore not only assist the student in utilizing his previously formed habits, but will also cause him to acquire new ones appropriate to the work he is to perform.

(3) *Accuracy.* No form of work is to be adopted which may lead to inaccurate habits of language-using, for habit-forming without accuracy means the forming of bad habits.

(4) *Gradation.* The teacher will cause the student to pass from the known to the unknown by easy stages, each of which will serve as a preparation for the next, and thereby secure a constantly increasing rate of progress.

(5) *Proportion.* The various aspects of language (i.e. understanding, speaking, reading, and writing) as well as the various branches of the study (i.e. phonetics, orthography, etymology, syntax, and semantics) to receive an appropriate measure of attention.

(6) *Concreteness.* The student will proceed from the concrete to the abstract, and will therefore be furnished with an abundance of well-chosen examples.

(7) *Interest.* The methods are to be devised in such a way that the interest of the student is always secured, for without interest there can be little progress.

(8) *Order of Progression.* The student should first be taught to hear and to articulate correctly, then to use sentences, then to make sentences, then to make (i.e. to inflect or to derive) words. In this way he will secure rapid and yet permanent results.

(9) *Multiple Line of Approach.* The language should be approached simultaneously from many different sides in many different ways, by means of many different forms of work.

Textbooks may differ in the sort of material supplied; teachers may differ in their mode of presentation; there will be room for individuality and personality. For years to come we shall not secure perfect uniformity and ideal results, but if these nine essential principles are understood and reasonably well observed by the method-writer, course-designer, and teacher, the resultant teaching is bound to be good and the results are bound to be satisfactory.

CHAPTER 7

Initial preparation

In the first chapter we have seen that each of us, child or adult, possesses in either an active or a latent stage certain capacities for the spontaneous assimilation of the spoken and colloquial form of any given language, native or foreign. In the case of the young child, these capacities are in an active state and at his immediate service, he does not require to be trained in their use; in the case of the average adult, these capacities are in a latent state, they have fallen into disuse, they are not at his immediate service, he must train himself to use them, he must learn how to learn.

In the first place, he must realize that language-learning (within the scope of our definition) is an *art* and not a *science*; to become proficient in an *art* is to acquire the capacity for *doing* something; to become proficient in a *science* is to acquire *knowledge* concerning something. So long as the student treats language-study as a science he will make little or no progress in the art of using language.

Now, there are two possible ways of acquiring proficiency in an art; the one consists in applying theory, the other consists in persistent efforts to imitate the successful performances of others. Let us say that the student wishes to use the French equivalent of 'she went'. By the method of theory he will remember that past actions are generally expressed by the French *passé indéfini* (or *perfect*); he will then remember that this tense is formed by means of one of the two auxiliaries plus the past participle. His knowledge of theory will tell him to derive from the infinitive *aller* the past participle *allé*; theory will also tell him that this particular verb requires the auxiliary *être* and not *avoir*, and that the present tense third person singular of

40

être is *est*. If he is writing the sentence, he must remember that the participle must in this case agree with the subject and be spelt *allée*.

By the method of practice he will merely reproduce by imitation the sentence *elle est allée*, which sentence he will have had occasions of learning or of reading. In both cases there is the possibility of error; the theory may be imperfectly known and one or more links in the chain of reasoning may be weak, or the sentence may have been badly memorized.

First attempts at imitation are sometimes inaccurate; our initial attempts at reproducing are occasionally unsuccessful; we wish to produce a foreign sound we have just heard, but utter a native sound instead; we wish to produce a foreign sentence, but construct it wrongly; we wish to express a certain thought, and fail to hit upon the right word. For this reason the method of practice is often termed *the method of trial and error*. We are told that some of our efforts will be successful and others unsuccessful, and that in the course of practice we shall gradually eliminate the unsuccessful ones. We are even told that it is only by making mistakes that we learn not to make them. Although we may admit a modicum of truth in this somewhat hyperbolical dictum, we would suggest that it is liable to misinterpretation. Nor is the term *trial and error* an ideal one from the language-teacher's point of view.

In both cases there is an implication that all successful attempts must necessarily be preceded by unsuccessful ones, which is not only untrue but unsound pedagogy. The literal interpretation of the term and doctrine may induce a sort of fatalistic attitude, and the principle of *accuracy* (which we shall deal with later) will suffer in consequence. It may provide teacher and student with an easy pretext to condone careless work. The student may say, 'Since it appears that error must precede perfection, I will not unduly strive towards accuracy.' The teacher may say, 'Since psychologists tell us that error is inevitable, I will allow my pupil to do inaccurate work.'

It may be true that some forms of inaccuracy in certain conditions tend to eliminate themselves in the course of time and practice, but it is certainly true that errors also tend to become habitual, and no psychologist has ever maintained that the forming of *bad* habits is a necessary step towards the acquisition of good ones. We would lay stress on this point, for there seems to be a real danger in the misapplication of such terms as 'trial and error', 'the selection of the successful and the rejection of the unsuccessful efforts', 'practice makes perfect', etc. Misunderstanding on this point has caused many teachers to encourage, and many students to acquire, pidgin-speech, and to consider it as the inevitable or even indispensable prelude to normal speech.

In the present chapter we are inquiring what are the processes of nature and how we may train the student to observe them. We have just seen that there is a method of theory and a method of practice; it is fairly evident that the latter is a natural process and that the former is not. We will now proceed to set forth another pair of rival processes and determine which is the one followed by the natural language-teaching forces.

When we are young we form new habits with facility; a new sort of work has to be performed, and we proceed to acquire the new habit which will enable us to perform it. When we are older we form new habits with greater difficulty and certainly with greater reluctance. We make all sorts of efforts (generally unconsciously) to avoid forming a new habit, for in some respects the adult seems to dread novelty.

A new sort of work has to be performed, and instead of acquiring the new habit or habits which will perform it we select habits already formed and strive to make them do the new work. Let us take a few examples in order to realize what this means. Suppose we wish to make Chinese characters with a native writing-brush. This is a new sort of work; in order to do it successfully we must hold the brush vertically in a way we have never held a brush before; we must form a new brush-holding and brush-using habit. But the average European adult will strive to use the brush and to trace the characters by holding the brush as he holds a pen; he will be using the known pen-holding habit instead of acquiring the unknown habit of holding a writing-brush.

Or we wish to learn to pronounce the vowel generally represented in French by *é*. This will require a muscular habit unknown to the average Englishman. What does he do? He seeks immediately to replace the required new effort by a known effort—and replaces the French *é* by the English *ay*. If this is too unsatisfactory he will strive to modify his *ay* until it seems to resemble sufficiently the required sound. Similarly, he will substitute for French *au, u,* or *on,* English *o* (as in 'boat'), *ew* (as in 'new'), and *ong*.

Or the English adult student may wish to learn to use French word-groups or sentences, in which case we shall almost invariably find that he only learns to use those which correspond most nearly to English constructions; he prefers to adapt his known syntax-habits rather than form new ones.

Now children have not this same reluctance to form new habits, either because their minds are more plastic, i.e. they are so used to forming new habits that a few more do not incommode them, or because they are not clever or intelligent enough to make the necessary selection from their stock of acquired habits.

Language-learning is essentially a habit-forming process, a process during which we must acquire *new* habits. It is, then, one of the cases where we cannot always proceed from the known to the unknown in the more obvious sense of the term; we must often consent to plunge (or be plunged) straight into the unknown.

The most important thing we have to do, then, is to train the student to form new habits and to cause him to refrain from adapting his old ones in cases where we know that such adaptation will be fruitless. We make this last qualification advisedly, because there are certain cases where successful adaptation is possible. A foreign language is not wholly different from our own tongue, and where identity exists obviously no new habit is required. (We must, however, see that the student selects the *right* previously acquired habit, that is to say, the *nearest* native equivalent.)

The capacity of forming new habits of observation, articulation, inflexion, compounding, or expression for every new language is one of our spontaneous capacities, and the student must when necessary be taught to form such new habits.

Another very characteristic feature of the natural process is *unconscious assimilation*; we learn without knowing that we are learning. What we therefore have to do is to train ourselves (or our students) *consciously* to learn *unconsciously*; we must set out deliberately to inhibit our capacities for focusing or concentrating our attention on the language-material itself. Attention must be given to what we want to say and not to the way we say it.

How shall we do it?

In the first place we must set out to sharpen our powers of receiving and retaining knowledge communicated to us orally. This may be difficult; we have become so accustomed to acquiring information from the written word *via* the eyes that we feel very bewildered and incapable when deprived of this medium. We hear a foreign word or sentence, and this auditory impression is such a rapid and transitory one that we feel that we cannot possibly retain it in our memory; we feel that we require at least one good look at the word so that we may hereafter reproduce in our imagination the written form. But we must resist this tendency; we must discipline ourselves to forego this artificial aid to memory, for ear-memory cannot be cultivated while we are visualizing. If we truly desire to tap the natural language-learning energies we must obey nature; we must train and drill our ears to do the work for which they were intended. If we make up our minds to train our ears to be efficient instruments we can do so: a little patience, a little practice, and we shall surely regain the power that we had allowed to lapse.

The exercises we use in order to sharpen our ear-perceptions and to make them serve us may be termed 'ear-training exercises'. This term may not satisfy those who delight in hair-splitting definitions; they may say, 'We cannot train our ears, but we can train our capacities for using them'; but the term is sufficiently accurate to designate what we mean it to designate.

How are ear-training exercises performed? There are several varieties. The simplest of all is this: the teacher articulates various sounds, either singly or in combination with others; we listen to these sounds and make unconscious efforts to reproduce them by saying them to ourselves. This is the most passive and most natural form of ear-training; we did it years ago when lying in our cradles listening to the sounds made by the people around us. If the teacher systematizes his work, so much the easier will it be for us who are training our ears.

We must then seek to recognize or identify certain sounds and to distinguish them from others. The teacher may write (in conventional phonetic symbols) a series of sounds on the blackboard and append to each a conventional number. He will articulate a sound and ask us to give him the number pertaining to it, or we may go up to the blackboard and point to the sound we think we have heard, or he may give us 'phonetic dictation', in which case he will articulate sounds which we must write down by means of these conventional phonetic symbols. This latter process has the advantage that it can subsequently be extended to the dictation of syllables or words.[1]

Other forms of ear-training exercises may be devised by those

[1] It will be preferable for these to be 'nonsense words', that is to say, artificial words with no meaning, for if real known words are articulated to us we may possibly write down not the sounds that we really hear but some sort of ingenious phonetic transliteration of the orthographic form of the word.

45

who are engaged in carrying out such work, care being taken that such exercises do really train the *ears* and not our capacities for successful guessing.

If you wish to know to what extent such exercises do have the desired effect, go through a short course of ear-training on these lines and you will yourself be a witness to their efficacy.

Ear-training is not confined to isolated sounds and simple combinations of sounds; it also includes the exercises of our capacities for perceiving or retaining long strings of syllables such as sentences. We are able to do this in the case of our mother-tongue, and there is no reason why we should not soon become fairly proficient in doing it in the case of a foreign language.

The next thing in importance is to learn how to articulate foreign sounds, singly, in simple combinations, or in long strings of syllables. We must train our mouth and our vocal organs generally; in some cases we must develop certain muscles in order that they may do easily and rapidly what is required of them. We have learnt to do this in the case of our mother-tongue, and we can learn to do the same for sounds which are so far unknown to us. It is never too late in life to develop a muscle in order that it may perform the small amount of work which will be required of it. We must go through a course of mouth-gymnastics; if we are disinclined to do so it means that we are disinclined to take the trouble to tap our natural language-learning resources.

What are articulation exercises? Like ear-training exercises, they exist in many varieties. We begin by practising on known sounds. We take simple sounds and learn to prolong them for a few seconds or to utter them rapidly, and we practise them in new and unfamiliar combinations. We are shown how to convert voiced into voiceless sounds and *vice versa*; we are taught how to produce sounds which are intermediate between two known sounds; we are shown how to convert known sounds into their nasal, lip-rounded, or palatalized forms, etc.;

46

we are trained to imitate strange noises of all sorts, and the phonetician is ready to show us how to make them. Our ear-training exercises will be of assistance to us, for it is easier to articulate sounds that we recognize than sounds which have so far been unfamiliar to our ears.

At a more advanced stage, articulation exercises gradually become merged into 'fluency exercises'. When we are asked to articulate a given string of syllables so many times in so many seconds we are learning to become fluent, to connect sound with sound and syllable with syllable without ugly gaps and awkward hesitations.

While ear-training and articulation exercises are being carried on the student should be encouraged to develop his powers of mimicry; after having heard on many different occasions words or strings of words uttered by the teacher he should strive to become at least as proficient as parrots and phonograph records in reproducing them spontaneously. The term *imitation* is not adequate to express the process by which he should work; what we require is absolute *mimicry*. Sounds, with all that appertains to them—pitch, timbre, length, abruptness, drawl, distinctness, and any other qualities and attributes possessed by them—should be mimicked faithfully and accurately; little or no distinction should be made by the learner between the characteristic pronunciation of the language he is learning and the personal pronunciation of his teacher. The teacher, indeed, should say to the student, 'Don't be content with a mere reproduction of what you imagine to be my standard of pronunciation; go further and mimic *me*.'

Ear-training, articulation, and mimicry exercises will carry us a long way towards our aim; when fairly proficient in these, we shall find little difficulty in *reproducing at first hearing a sentence which has been articulated to us*. This is one of our most important aims; once able to do this, we are able to avail ourselves immediately of one of the most valuable channels for acquiring the foreign language; we are able to assimilate foreign sentences by ear; every sentence repeated in our hearing will have its due effect in furthering our knowledge of the language and our capacity for using it.

Anyone who is unable to repeat with tolerable accuracy any sentence he has just heard is certainly unable to assimilate the foreign language by spontaneous methods. He may seek to compensate this inability by methods involving the imagery of the written word, but these methods will be unnatural ones and will inhibit the development of the spontaneous powers. Anyone who experiences a difficulty in repeating a foreign sentence which he has just heard will be severely handicapped in his subsequent work, for he will be paying attention to his hearing and articulation when he should be devoting his attention to other things. Indeed, we would go so far as to say that the power of correctly reproducing a string of syllables just heard is one of the essential things we must possess in order to make any real progress in the acquisition of the spoken language.

It is this power which enables us to memorize on a wide scale sentences and similar strings of words. Whether we like it or not, whether the prospect is encouraging or not, it is quite certain that an easy command of the spoken (and even of the written) language can only be gained by acquiring the absolute mastery of thousands of combinations, regular and irregular. We shall see later that certain forms of synthetic work exist which will enable us to form correctly an almost unlimited number of foreign sentences; we shall see that the utilizing of these studial forms of work will carry us very far on our way to acquire the language; but, ingenious and sound though they may be, they will not replace the cruder and more primitive process of memorizing integrally a vast number of word-groups.

Now this task cannot be accomplished by means of intensive and laborious repetition work; it cannot be accomplished by the traditional methods of memorizing; book-work and perseverance will never lead us to the goal of our memorizing ambitions.

As we shall see later, in the early stages a certain amount of deliberate and conscious memorizing must be done; we shall insist on the daily repetition of a certain number of useful compounds, but sooner or later we shall come to a stage in which memory-work must be carried out on a far larger scale and in a far more spontaneous manner. We must train ourselves to become spontaneous memorizers, and this can only be done in one way: we must acquire the capacity for retaining a chance phrase or compound which has fallen upon our ears in the course of a conversation or speech. It is in this way that we have acquired those thousands of phrases and combinations which make up the bulk of our daily speech in our own language. We have acquired the capacity of noting and retaining any new combinations of English words which we may chance to hear; we do this unconsciously, and are not aware of doing so; we rarely or never invent new types of compounds, but simply reproduce at appropriate moments those types of compounds which we have happened to hear used by those speaking in our presence. This is one of the habits we acquired in our infancy; this is one of the habits we must revive now and use for the foreign language we are studying. So long as we have not acquired this habit our progress will be slow—too slow for the purpose we have in view.

At a later stage of our study, it is true, we may make such acquisitions by *reading* instead of *listening*, but this will only be after we have become proficient in reproducing what we *hear*. We may be inclined to think that we assimilate new linguistic material by the eye alone, but this is not the case; the eye alone cannot assimilate. It may be taken as proved today that all normal people 'inner-articulate' all that they read, that we are indeed incapable of understanding what we read unless a process of 'inner-articulating' is going on at the same time. We need not stop at present to inquire exactly what is the psychological definition and explanation of this inner-articulating; we may content ourselves for the moment by defining this process as a sort of 'mental repetition'.[1] It is well known that deaf-mute children who have been taught to read and to write never acquire the power of writing their 'native language' as normally used; they produce an artificial variety which reads as if it were written by a foreigner. Nor is this to be wondered at; it is perfectly in accordance with what might be expected; deaf-mutes cannot articulate, either aloud or mentally; they are therefore compelled to learn by studial method, and they acquire language as slowly and as painfully as anyone acquires a foreign language by mere studial methods.

To learn to repeat mentally exactly what we hear, neither more nor less, without the intervention of any other elements than those of hearing and articulating, is, then, one of the things we must do if we wish to avail ourselves of the help which nature is ready to afford us.

Another of the spontaneous capacities with which we are endowed is that of understanding the gist of what we hear without any intervention of analysis or synthesis. Some people seem never to have lost this power. It suffices that they should have a certain number of opportunities of listening to the language being used for them to be able to gather the general sense of what they hear. Others do not appear to possess this 'gift'; they cannot understand anything they have not analysed and reduced to its component units. In reality, if they would refrain from so analysing what they hear (or even read) they would soon find themselves able to do as well in this respect as the 'gifted'. We therefore suggest that a programme of this sort should include a certain number of exercises designed expressly to develop this power of direct understanding.

What sort of exercises should these be? They are many and varied. The essential feature should be the rigid exclusion of all opportunities for reasoning, calculation, analysis, or synthesis.

[1] Victor Egger, La Parole intérieure: 'Souvent ce que nous appelons entendre comprend un commencement d'articulation silencieuse, des mouvements faibles, ébauchés, dans l'appareil vocal' (Ribot).

The pupil must not be allowed to focus his consciousness on the structure of the language; he must keep his attention on the subject-matter. The natural law in this respect would seem to be that we shall come to understand what we hear provided that we fix our minds not on the actual words used but on the circumstances which result in the words in question. Interest must be present. If you are not interested directly or indirectly in what you hear, you may listen and listen for months or even years without understanding what you hear. If, on the other hand, things are said in your presence concerning matters which affect even distantly your welfare or which are connected with your interests or surroundings, you will have a tendency to grasp the meaning of what is said. We must endeavour to devise a series of exercises which fulfil these conditions; we must design forms of work in which the student's attention shall be directed towards the subject-matter and away from the form in which it is expressed. Gradation, however, must be observed if we wish to obtain fairly rapid results, we must first work with a comparatively limited vocabulary, we must use an abundance of gesture, we must avail ourselves of everything likely to further our aim. In so doing, however, we must avoid the other extreme; if we are too careful in our choice of words, if we speak too slowly and over-emphasize our speech, the process of understanding will be too conscious; we shall be fostering habits of conscious study and of focused attention, things which are very good in their way, but which are not calculated to further the particular end we have at present in view.

The most natural form of work, indeed the first form of work which suggests itself to us, consists in talking to our pupils, talking to them naturally and fluently, talking to them about anything which may conceivably be of interest to them. We may show them the different parts of the room in which the lessons are given, the furniture, objects on the table or in our pockets, and while showing them we name them and speak about them.

We may perform all sorts of actions and say what we are doing; we may describe the position of the various objects, their qualities and attributes; we may show pictures and describe them. These elementary talks will gradually develop; we may pass by easier stages from the concrete to the abstract; in the end we shall be relating (and even reading) simple stories, and our listeners will come to follow our thoughts and understand what we are saying, even as we understood the simple stories for which we clamoured in our nursery days.

Another form of work, called 'imperative drill', consists in giving orders in the foreign language to the pupils to perform certain actions (stand up, sit down, take your book, open it, shut it, etc.). In the initial stage such orders will be accompanied by the necessary gestures; the students will not be slow to grasp what is required of them, and in a very short time they will respond automatically to the stimulus provided by the foreign imperative sentence.

Another form of exercise designed to cultivate the capacity of immediate comprehension is that in which we require our pupils to answer yes or no (*oui* or *non*, *ja* or *nein*, etc.) to hundreds of questions which we ask them. (Is this your book? Is the sky blue? Am I speaking to you? Are we in France? etc.)

Certain other simple forms of systematic *questionnaire* exercises will further develop the natural powers of comprehension, of associating the word with the thought. A type of exercise called 'action-drill' will have the same effect if carried out as a means to the particular end we have in view.

These then are the chief things to be done once we have decided to enlist on our behalf the universal and natural powers of language-using, and these are some of the various ways in which may achieve our aim. All of them are possible and all of them can be carried out in actual practice by any teacher who has a sufficient command of the foreign language (and if he has not, we can hardly call him a competent teacher). Nothing has been suggested here which has not already been successfully carried out by those whose business it is to ascertain experimentally how languages are actually learned.

The initial stages of the language-course will be very largely characterized by these forms of work, in order that the student may be thoroughly prepared and mentally equipped for the later stages.

CHAPTER **8**

Habit-forming and habit-adapting

Language-learning, like all other arts as contrasted with sciences, is a habit-forming process. Proficiency in the understanding of the structure of a language is attained by treating the subject as a *science*, by studying the *theory*; but proficiency in the *use* of a language can only come as a result of perfectly formed habits. No foreign word, form, or combination of these is 'known' or 'mastered' until we can use it automatically, until we can attach it to its meaning without conscious analysis, until we can produce it without hesitation and conscious synthesis. We hear a foreign sentence as pronounced at a normal speed by a native speaker. If we understand this sentence as soon as it falls from his lips, if we understand it without being conscious of its form or without even realizing that we are listening to a foreign language, we 'possess' that sentence, it forms part of the material which we have gained as the result of a habit; our understanding of it is '*automatic*'. If, on the other hand, we ask the speaker to repeat it or to say it more slowly, if we claim a moment of reflection in order to realize the parts of which it is composed, if we subject it to a rapid analysis or to a rapid translation, we do not possess the sentence; it has not become automatic.

We wish to speak; if the foreign sentence springs to our lips as soon as we have formulated the thought, if we are unconscious of the words or the form of the words contained in it, if we are unaware of the manner in which we have pieced it together, it is certain that we have produced it automatically, we have produced it as the result of a perfectly formed habit. If, on the other hand, we prepare the sentence in advance; if, as we utter it, we consciously choose the words or the form of the

54

words contained in it; if we build it up by conscious synthesis or by a rapid translation from an equivalent sentence of our native tongue, we do not produce it automatically; we have not formed the habit of using the sentence or the type of sentence to which it belongs; we are producing it by means of conscious calculation.

Adult students in general dislike forming new habits and avoid such work as far as possible; they seek to replace it by forms of study requiring discrimination and other processes of the intellect. One reason for this is that habit-forming often entails monotonous work, whereas the other types of work are more or less interesting; another reason is that the forming of a habit seems a slow process; so many repetitions are required and progress is not at once apparent, whereas the other form of work has all the appearance of rapidity. We know, however, that in reality what we have learnt as the result of a habit is not only immediately available at all times, but is also a permanent acquisition, and that what we have learnt by the aid of theory alone is neither immediately available nor permanent. Let us take an example to illustrate our point.

We wish to learn when and how to use each of the German cases. The theory of the declension provides us with all the necessary rules and exceptions. One set of prepositions requires the accusative, another the dative, another the genitive, another accusative or dative according to certain semantic considerations. This rule can be mastered without any great difficulty; within the space of a few hours the necessary formulas may be committed to memory, and the student imagines that the problem is solved for all time. 'Whenever I want to know what case to use', he thinks, 'I shall only have to remember to which category the preposition belongs and I shall know what case is required.' In reality his knowledge of the theory, i.e. his memory of the categories, will soon become blurred and will tend to fade away; and even if he does succeed in retaining this fresh in his memory, he will always require a second or two of

55

conscious reflection before he is able to hit on the right case. He will be using consciousness where unconsciousness would serve him better; if (as is probable) he has learnt to determine gender by a similar process, his conscious attention will have to be devoted to this as well, he will be focusing his attention on the language-material, which will prevent him from focusing it on the things he wishes to say. Deciding to use these 'short cuts' he will therefore assume for his whole lifetime the burden of continual conscious effort.

Now, instead of learning and applying theory he might memorize a hundred or so real living sentences, each exemplifying one of the results of the theory. By doing so he would acquire a hundred or so new habits or automatic actions. He recoils before the task; the perfect memorizing of a simple sentence is so distasteful to him; it seems to take so long; he fails to realize the permanent advantages which he might obtain by doing it; he chooses what seems the easier path, the short cut.

It is here that we see the value of spontaneous assimilation. If the student has trained his capacities of retaining unconsciously what he may happen to hear (or read), he will memorize without effort, and without the expenditure of any appreciable amount of nervous energy.

The same considerations apply to the learning of the French conjugation, English pronunciation, Hungarian vocalic harmony, Welsh mutation, or to the overcoming of the other obstacles in the path of progress towards perfect attainment.

The fear of monotonous and tedious memorizing work, and the realization of the length of time necessary for each act of memorizing, induces the student to invent pretexts for avoiding such work. He declares that 'parrot-work' is not education, that modern educationalists condemn 'learning by rote', that the age of blind repetition is over and that the age of intelligent understanding has taken its place. He will talk of the method of discovery, the factor of interest, and will even quote to us 'the laws of nature' in defence of his thesis. But we know that in reality these are but so many excuses for his disinclination to form those habits which can secure him the automatism which alone will result in sound and permanent progress.

This fear of tediousness is not really justified at all, for mechanical work is not necessarily monotonous. Automatism, it is true, is acquired by repetition, but this repetition need not be of the parrot-like type. Repetition, in the sense ascribed to it by the psychologist, simply means having many separate occasions to hear, to see, to utter, or to write a given word or sentence. The object of most of the language-teaching exercises, drills, and devices invented or developed in recent years is precisely to ensure proper repetition in attractive and interesting ways.

Nearly all the time spent by the teacher in explaining why such and such a form is used and why a certain sentence is constructed in a certain way is time lost, for such explanations merely appease curiosity; they do not help us to form new habits, they do not develop automatism. Those who have learnt to use the foreign language and who do use it successfully have long since forgotten the why and the wherefore; they can no longer quote to you the theory which was supposed to have procured them their command of the language.

When teaching the French word *chauve-souris* it is not necessary to point out that this is literally equivalent to 'bald-mouse'; and if we tell our student that *ça se comprend* really means 'that understands itself', we are telling him something which is not true, and something that will cause him needless perplexity. *Hauptstadt* is the German equivalent of 'capital' (in the geographical sense), and we need not pander to morbid etymological habits by making an allusion to 'head-town'. Nothing is gained, but much is lost, if we tell the student that the French say 'I am become' instead of 'I have become'.

It may be objected that habit-forming is aided by these explanations, that the knowledge of the why and the wherefore

THE PRINCIPLES OF LANGUAGE-STUDY

is a useful aid to the process of memorizing. There is something to be said for this statement; we are ready to admit that in some instances it is good to point out the nature of the laws that stand behind the sentences which exemplify them; we shall even show later in what cases and for what reasons we counsel the giving of explanations. But we are entirely at issue with those who maintain that explanations are an indispensable concomitant of memorizing, and we give a flat contradiction to those who maintain that 'they cannot memorize what they don't understand'. The most successful linguists have attained their proficiency by memorizing sentences they could not analyse. The temptation to replace habit-forming by analysis and synthesis is so strong that the teacher must continually react against it.

As we have already seen, instead of acquiring the habit of using the French sound *é* the English student persists in replacing it by some form of the English *ay*; conversely, the French student of English tends to replace the English *ay* by the French *é*. Most of these acts of substitution are illegitimate; French *eu* is a very poor substitute for English *u* in *but*, but the English word *air* is a mere caricature of the French word *air;* of the six sounds contained in the word *thoroughly* /θʌrəli/, only two, /ə/ and /l/, are in any way equivalent to French sounds. About half of the forty-six sounds (or rather 'phones') contained in the English phonetic system have no equivalent in French, and about the same proportion of the thirty-seven French sounds are absent from English. Yet most French users of English and most English users of French endeavour respectively to speak the foreign language with no other sounds than their native sounds. The French system of stress and intonation is entirely different from the English system, but most English students will use their native system when speaking French. The average English student replaces French habits of sentence-building by his previously acquired English habits, and also attributes to French words or word-compounds the

58

meanings (or connotations) possessed by what he imagines to be their English equivalents.

In many cases he is undoubtedly justified; his efforts are not all misplaced; some foreign sounds *are* actually identical with some native sounds, some foreign constructions *are* actually parallel with some native constructions, and some foreign words and expressions *do* possess an exact counterpart in the native language. But the trouble is that the student fails to realize in what cases these identities exist; untrained in observation and discrimination, he considers as equivalents things which are not, and fails to identify as equivalents things which are. French *a* in *patte* is frequently not far removed from a perfectly English variety of *u* in *cut*, but the average Frenchman pronounces *cut* with the French vowel *eu* in *veuve*, and the average Englishman pronounces *patte* either with the vowel of *pat* or of *part*. The last syllable of *pleasure* is practically identical with the French word *je*, but the average Frenchman does not know this, and substitutes some sort of French *ure* or *eure*. The French words *souhaite, semelle, laine, dialecte* are very similar to the (real or imaginary) English words *sweat, smell, len, d'yullect*, but the average English student does not know this, and uses pronunciations such as *soohate, semell, lane, dee-ah-lect* instead.

In these and all parallel cases the student is utilizing certain of his previously acquired habits, but unfortunately he has selected the wrong ones instead of the right ones; it is for the skilful language-teacher to ascertain which of the student's known habits can be most nearly adapted to what is required.

The same thing holds good in the case of construction, choice of words, etc. The English student constructs the sentence *Je marcherai à la gare* on the wrong model; if he must use an English habit at all, he should in this case proceed from *I shall go on foot to the station* and not from *I shall walk to the station*. Some may inquire at this point, 'Why drag in English at all? Why not think in the foreign language without reference to the mother tongue?' We would reply that this is hardly relevant to the matter under immediate consideration; we are simply showing that the average student, if left to himself, will tend not only to utilize his native linguistic habits, but to select very unsuitable ones. We would, however, add that cases do undoubtedly exist in which the student would be well advised to enlist some of his previously acquired habits; a judiciously selected native form will produce better results than a badly constructed foreign form.[1]

[1] A typical example has just been noticed by the writer: a Dutch student's pronunciation of 'know it' was almost unintelligible, but when advised to replace this rendering by the Dutch word *nooit* he produced a very close approximation to the English pronunciation.

CHAPTER 9

Accuracy

Let us be quite sure we understand what we mean by the term 'accuracy'. There is, of course, no such thing as intrinsic or unconditioned accuracy; the term is a relative and not an absolute one; this word, and its synonyms 'correctness', 'rightness', and the adjectives 'accurate', 'correct', 'right', 'good', 'proper', etc., all imply *conformity with a given standard or model*. If the dialect we are learning is an unclassical one, differing appreciably from the literary form, then accuracy will consist, among other things, in not using the literary or traditionally correct forms. Therefore, if we are learning colloquial French we shall be guilty of inaccuracies every time we use *cela* instead of *ça* and every time we use the *passé défini* (or whatever the present name of this tense may be) or the *imparfait du subjonctif*. Whether the French Academician approves of the colloquial forms does not concern us from the moment that we have set out to learn the colloquial forms. *Du bon pain, c'est pas ça, i' m'a dit que'qu'chose* may or may not be typical of educated speech, but if, for reasons of our own, we have decided to acquire the type of speech exemplified, then *de bon pain, ce n'est pas cela, il m'a dit quelque chose* will be inaccurate as not being in conformity with the standard we have chosen.

Who do you give it to? What have you got? It's me, Under the circumstances, etc., may or may not represent an atrocious English dialect; but we may decide to teach this dialect to our foreign students, if only because this is the dialect most often used by the average educated speaker. Once we have made this decision we shall consider as inaccuracies such forms as *To whom do you give it? What have you? It is I, In the circumstances*.

When, therefore, we use the terms *inaccuracy, mistake, fault, wrong form, error*, etc., we shall always mean *something not in conformity with the type of speech chosen as a convenient standard*.

One of the duties of the language-teacher and method-writer is to react against the tendency of the student towards inaccuracy. We shall generally find two types of inaccuracy: (*a*) that which consists in using the wrong dialect (literary instead of colloquial, or *vice versa*), and (*b*) that which consists in using pidgin. Pidgin or pidgin-speech may be defined as that variety of a language which is used exclusively by foreigners.[1] Some kinds of pidgin (e.g. pidgin-English of the China ports, the Chinook jargon of British Columbia) have become so standardized that they may almost be considered as normal languages; many people deliberately set out to learn such pidgin-languages, and we may conceive of the possibility of these possessing sub-pidgin forms.

In connexion with the first type of inaccuracy (wrong dialect), we should here note that the uneducated native tends to make too extensive a use of the popular dialect, whereas the tendency of the student to whom the language is foreign is the contrary one: he makes too extensive a use of the classical or traditionally correct form. The uneducated native will tend to use the colloquial form when writing; the foreigner will tend to use the literary when speaking. In both cases it is part of the functions of the teacher to react against these tendencies: to the schoolchild he will say, 'Don't use a preposition to finish a sentence with!'; to the foreign speaker he will give the contrary advice.

Having defined the terms *accuracy* and *inaccuracy*, let us now see to how many branches of language-study these terms (and their synonyms) may be applied.

(*a*) There may be accuracy or inaccuracy in *sounds*. The student must be taught, by means of appropriate drills and exercises, to make and to use the sounds of the language he is

[1] Or, in some cases, by natives when speaking to foreigners.

studying; if he uses an English sound in place of a French one, or if he uses a right French sound in the wrong place, he will be doing inaccurate work. Ear-training and articulation exercises (as described in Chapter 7) will tend to make him accurate in this respect.

(*b*) There may be accuracy or inaccuracy in the use of *stress* and *intonation*. To use one language with the stress and intonation system of another results in a form of pidgin. The student must be taught, by means of appropriate drills and exercises, to observe and to imitate the system used by the natives.

(*c*) There may be accuracy or inaccuracy in fluency. Most languages are spoken at the rate of five syllables per second. Nothing is to be gained by speaking at a slower rate; indeed, it will often be found that rapid speech is easier of acquisition than slow speech. Correct fluency includes correct assimilation or absence of assimilation, and the requisite degree of smoothness or grace of utterance; we may often note the harsh and halting effect of the speech of foreigners who, when speaking their native tongue, are masters of the art of elocution. By means of appropriate exercises, the student can be made to observe accuracy in fluency.

(*d*) When the student uses the traditional spelling of the language he should be encouraged to avoid orthographic inaccuracy. Generally, however, few mistakes of this sort are made, and these tend to be eliminated more or less spontaneously. If this is not the case, appropriate exercises may be devised in order to ensure accuracy in this respect. Let us note here, with all the emphasis which is due to such an important point, that the exclusive use of a phonetic script in the early stages generally leads to a greater accuracy in the traditional spelling which is learnt subsequently. We make no attempt here to furnish an explanation of why and how this is so, but leave it to psychologists to investigate the subject and to ascertain the causes of what may seem paradoxical and even incredible to those who have not had sufficient teaching experience.

(*e*) There may be accuracy or inaccuracy in *combining words*; the laws of sentence-building are not the same for all languages, and the student must be trained to observe the right laws; he must be taught to be accurate in concord, in compounding, and in word-order. Some of the most interesting methods and devices are designed specifically to react against inaccurate tendencies in this respect. It is as easy and as natural to say *la table* (and not *le table*) as it is to say *latitude* (and not *letitude*); it is as easy to learn *je ne le lui ai pas donné* as any of the inaccurate examples of word-order by which the average English student tends to replace it.

(*f*) There may be accuracy or inaccuracy in the use of *inflexions*. It is as important to learn the right inflected forms of a word as to learn the uninflected word. If our methods are right, it is as easy to learn the word *enverrai* as it is to learn the word *envoyer*, and far easier to learn *enverrai* than *envoyerai*. The habit of using the right inflexions is one that must be acquired at as early a stage as possible and as unconsciously as possible. Many methods and devices exist which have been designed to combat inaccuracy in this respect.

(*g*) There may be accuracy or inaccuracy in *meanings*. The meaning of a word may vary considerably according to its context. *Open* in the sense of *open the door* has not the same meaning as *open* in the sense of *open the box*. Most English words have two or more meanings; the foreign words which are assumed to be their equivalents may also have two or more meanings, but the foreign word does not necessarily have all the meanings of the English word, and *vice versa*. The branch of linguistics which deals with meanings, synonyms, translations, definitions, etc., is called 'semantics'; special forms of work have been devised to ensure semantic accuracy on the part of the student.

The principle of accuracy may be expressed as follows: *Do not allow the student to have opportunities for inaccurate work until he has arrived at the stage at which accurate work is to be reasonably expected.*

If we force him to speak French before he has been sufficiently drilled in French sounds, we are forcing him to pronounce inaccurately. If we tell him to do French composition before he has acquired the necessary habits of inflexion, compounding, and sentence-building, we are inviting him to do inaccurate work. If we compel him to talk to us in French before he has become proficient in conversion and similar drills, we are virtually compelling him to speak pidgin-French and, incidentally, to form the habit of doing so. In opposition to the principle of accuracy, we are frequently told that 'It is only by making mistakes that we learn not to make them,' and that 'Only by going into the water can we learn to swim.' These are cheap proverbs, and we may as easily coin others such as: 'It is by making mistakes that we form the habit of making them'; or, 'He who has not learnt to swim will drown when thrown into deep water.'

The method of *trial and error*, to which we have already alluded, is in direct opposition to the principles of accuracy; it is the method of sink-or-swim, of die-or-survive, of flounder-and-grope-until-you-hit-on-the-right-way. To replace this method by something less cruel is the function of such things as guides, teachers, and pedagogic devices. For let us remark that the environment of the young child who acquires language spontaneously, as explained in Chapter 1, is such that error has little or no chance of surviving; the persons with whom he is in contact are providing him continually with accurate models of whatever the dialect may happen to be; he is given no chance of imitating wrong models, and he is not intelligent enough to create them himself in any appreciable degree. Furthermore, the young child as a matter of fact does not begin to use language until he is fairly proficient in the important speech-habits; he rarely or never uses a form of speech until he has memorized it by hearing it used by others.

One of the most important advances in the art of language-teaching will have been made when the principle of accuracy is understood, accepted, and adopted by all who are engaged in this work either as teachers or as trainers of teachers.

We have seen, then, that there are seven branches of language-study in which accuracy (or inaccuracy) may be developed. In connexion with each of these there exist methods, exercises, and devices designed to inculcate right habits and to prevent the formation of wrong ones. There exist also sciences upon which most of these are based. The methods dealing with sounds, stress, intonation, and fluency are based on the data furnished by phonetics, and without a knowledge of this science the teacher is unlikely to secure accuracy in these branches. The (so far empirical) science of grammar is the basis of those methods and exercises calculated to ensure accuracy in in-flexions and sentence-building. Orthography (possibly a science, though this is doubtful) is the basis of spelling work, and the new (and so far empirical) science of semantics will furnish the necessary data for all methods, exercises, and devices concerned with meanings.

In addition to these specific sciences, methods, exercises, and devices, there are general forms of method of the strategical order, the effect of which is to ensure general accuracy. As these are practically identical with gradation, we reserve their consideration for the next chapter.

CHAPTER 10

Gradation

Gradation means passing from the known to the unknown by easy stages, each of which serves as a preparation for the next. If a student who is willing to learn and is capable of learning finds his lessons too difficult, if he fails to understand or to apply correctly the explanations we give him, if his rate of progress is too slow, if he forgets frequently what he has already learnt, and if his oral or written work is characterized by an excessive degree of inaccuracy, it is perfectly certain that his course and his lessons are badly graded.

The student's progress may in the initial stage be slow; after ten or twenty lessons he may not seem to have advanced very far; but if he has been laying a good foundation he has been doing good work, for it will mean that the next stage of his work will be accomplished more easily and more rapidly. During the first lessons he is not so much learning the language as learning how to learn it. During the second period his progress will be more rapid and he will assimilate more of the actual language-material, and he will then be learning in such a way that the third stage will be still more rapid, and so on through the subsequent stages; his rate of progress will increase in proportion as he advances.

In the ideal course, this principle will be observed in the fullest possible measure; the course itself will be divided into appropriate stages, each of which will be marked by an increased capacity on the part of the student for assimilating and using language-material.

The vocabulary in a well-graded language-course will be arranged in such a manner that the more useful words will be learnt before the less useful. (Let us remember that there are two sorts of 'useful words'; those which are *useful in themselves* on account of their intrinsic meaning, and words which are *useful as sentence-formers*.) The rate of progress on the part of the student will depend very largely on the manner in which the vocabulary is graded. Twenty-five well-chosen words will form more useful sentences than many people believe; with 500 well-chosen words an incredibly large number of valuable sentences can be formed. For detailed information on this point we would refer the reader to the statistics which have been compiled by those who have made a special study of this particular subject. In the ideally graded course the student first assimilates a relatively small but exceedingly important vocabulary; he learns to use it, he learns the more important peculiarities of each word, he learns how to combine these words in sentences, he learns the exact range of meanings covered by each word either singly or in combination with its fellows. This small vocabulary then constitutes a sound nucleus, and this nucleus is of twofold utility; it not only provides the student with useful words, with language-material which he can actually use, but it serves at the same time as a sort of centre of attraction for new language-material. The most apt illustration of this form of gradation is the snowball, the huge mass of snow which accumulates rapidly and easily once we have provided the nucleus represented by the first compact and well-rounded handful.

The grammatical material must also be graded. Certain moods and tenses are more useful than others; let us therefore concentrate on the useful ones first. In a language possessing a number of cases, we will not learn off the whole set of prepositions, their uses and requirements, but we will select them in accordance with their degree of importance. As for lists of rules and exceptions, if we learn them at all we will learn them in strict order of necessity. In most languages we shall probably find certain fundamental laws of grammar and syntax upon which the whole structure of the language depends; if our course is to comprise the conscious study of the mechanism of a given language, then, in accordance with the principle of gradation, let us first learn these essentials and leave the details to a later stage.

Gradation can and must also be observed in the study of the semantic aspect of a language. If a given word has several meanings, let us first associate the word with its more usual or useful meanings. If a foreigner is to learn the English verb *to afford*, let him begin by using it in such sentences as *I can't afford it*, and not in such examples as *It affords me the necessary opportunity*. If we are teaching French, let us first use *ciel* in the sense of *sky* and leave the idea of *heaven* to a later stage. *I may go* has more than one meaning, but let us first teach it in the sense of *Perhaps I shall go*; the other varieties are not of pressing importance. When we introduce *but*, let us associate it with its usual meaning and forget for the moment that semantic variety which is equivalent to *except*.

It is not sufficient for us to adopt the general principle of gradation; we must adopt the right sort of gradation; for we can easily imagine all sorts of false grading. We can imagine a teacher refusing, on the score of gradation, to teach irregular forms before regular ones, and justifying his procedure by the assertion that the regular is easy and the irregular difficult. This kind of gradation, however, is obviously unsound, seeing that some of the most useful words in most languages are very irregular. As a matter of fact, in a sound course of study based on the principle of automatism, the irregular forms are learnt as easily as (and sometimes more easily than) regular forms.

We can also imagine some teachers maintaining (on grounds of gradation) that the *word* should be treated before the *sentence*. They would say that it is easier to assimilate a word than a sentence, that what is easier should come first. Others might say, 'Teach easy words first and difficult ones later.' But this cannot be right, for if we observed this rule we should teach a

Spaniard or a Frenchman the English verb *to comprehend* before the verb *to understand*. Gradation does not necessarily imply passing from the easy to the difficult, but it always does imply passing from the more important, useful, or fundamental to the less important, useful, or fundamental. Now, whatever the true unit of speech may be, our leading semanticians and speech-psychologists are all agreed that this unit is rarely the word, but generally the word-group or sentence. Consequently, to start from the word is not only bad gradation but bad semantics.

We have heard it asserted on grounds of gradation that the *written* form of a language should be studied before its *spoken* form. Here again we find the same misinterpretation of the term gradation and the same fallacy of 'facility'. If relative facility is to be the basis of gradation, then we should teach the geography of Portugal before teaching the geography of the British Empire, and we should postpone our study of chess until we have become expert in the easier game of noughts and crosses. To learn how to read and to write a language may possibly be easier than to learn how to speak it and to understand it when spoken, but this has no bearing on the subject of gradation.

Another false interpretation of the principle is to assume that the student will begin by using incorrect or pidgin-French (or whatever the language may be) and will gradually become more perfect 'with practice' as he goes on. Now if this is gradation, it is a particularly vicious form, and in flat contradiction to the principles of habit-forming and accuracy.

To teach to adults 'child-like words' before the words used by adults is another misinterpretation of gradation. We do indeed see classes in which boys or girls of twelve or thirteen learn to recite foreign nursery rhymes, but we doubt whether any teacher would seriously maintain that words such as *dog* or *sheep* should be preceded by *bow-wow* or *baa-baa*.

Having examined some faulty and vicious manners of interpreting gradation, let us now proceed to epitomize a few rational applications of the principle we have set forth, and let us assure the reader that each one of these has been proved to be psychologically sound.

(a) *Ears before Eyes.* All fresh language-material should be presented in its oral form and not in its written form. Sounds should first be practised without any reference to any graphic forms of representation; the ear, not the eye, is the organ provided by nature for recognizing and assimilating sounds. Words should first be heard and imitated orally, for ideal assimilation is not helped but hindered when the written form is presented.

Fresh word-groups and sentences should also as far as possible be first introduced and learnt orally. The adult student who complains that the process is too difficult is under the illusion that we hear with our eyes.

(b) *Reception before Production.* It is quite certain that the student will be unable to reproduce a sound, a word, or a word-group that has been pronounced to him until he has really *heard* the model that he is called upon to imitate. There is a great difference between really hearing and merely imagining that one has heard a sound or a succession of sounds. As a rule we do not hear what is actually said to us; we merely hear what we expect to hear. Ask the average foreigner to repeat after you a word such as *und'stand*; instead of reproducing the exaggeratedly shortened form as represented above in two syllables, he will say *understand* in three syllables. As a matter of fact, he is under the impression that he heard you articulate the three syllables, and consequently he reproduces what he thought you said. Ask the average foreigner to repeat after you the word *turn* pronounced in southern English (i.e. without an *r*) and he will insert an *r* because he imagines that he heard one. The sentence *il doit venir* is pronounced by the average Frenchman as /idwavni:r/, pronounce it like that to the average English student of French and ask him to imitate you; in most cases you will obtain what the student imagined he heard, viz. /il dwa vɛniə/ (the last word having a remarkable resemblance to the English word *veneer*).

The student must therefore not only be trained to hear, but in all fairness to him he should be given ample opportunity of hearing the sound, word, or word-group that he will be called upon to reproduce. Let him hear it several times, let him concentrate his attention on the succession of sounds without any regard to its written form or its meaning. Let us endeavour as far as possible to give the student two or even more separate opportunities (with appropriate intervals) of truly hearing any given sound, word, or word-group before calling upon him to imitate the model.

(*c*) *Oral Repetition before Reading.* Just as oral repetition should be preceded by a period of audition, so should reading be preceded by oral repetition. Before calling upon a pupil to read off from the blackboard or his book a word, list of words, sentence, or succession of sentences, let us first ask him to repeat after us the required material. If he cannot reproduce to our satisfaction a sentence that he has just heard from our lips, he will certainly be unable to reproduce the sentence by the process of reading.

(*d*) *Immediate Memory before Prolonged Memory.* The teacher pronounces a sound or a succession of sounds (a word, a word-group, or a sentence). A few seconds later the pupil reproduces what he has heard; he does not find it very difficult to do so, for the sound of the teacher's voice is still ringing in his ears; in his imagination he can still hear the teacher's voice, and he has but to speak in unison with it. The sort of memory which enables him to reproduce what he has just heard is called *immediate memory.*

Another time the teacher pronounces a sound or a succession of sounds. The next day the pupil is called upon (without being prompted) to reproduce what he heard the day before. He may fail altogether to do so, or he may succeed. That sort of memory which enables him to reproduce what he has heard one, several, or many days before is called *prolonged memory*. Let us be quite certain that we understand the difference between these two extreme varieties of memory. Let us choose a word in a language unknown to us. Let this be the Hungarian word *szenvedni*, meaning *to suffer*. The word is pronounced /tsɛnvɛdni/; in the absence of a teacher let us pronounce the word ourselves three or four times. . . . Let us take our eyes from the book, and let a few seconds pass. . . . How do you say *to suffer* in Hungarian? /tsɛnvɛdni/. Quite correct; we have reproduced the word from immediate memory. Tomorrow or the day after let us ask ourselves how they express *to suffer* in Hungarian. If we are able to answer correctly without referring to the book, it will be by dint of our *prolonged memory*. If this experiment is inconclusive, let us take a word-group, a sentence, or a list of words; we shall then realize how much more difficult it is to reproduce new matter after the sound of it has faded from our ears.

Let us remember this experiment when we are teaching; when our pupils reproduce correctly (either by repetition or by translation) what they have heard a few seconds (or even a few minutes) before, let us remember that we have so far only appealed to their immediate memory, and let us not expect an equally satisfactory result when we call upon them to reproduce the same matter the next day without prompting. To expect the same results from the prolonged as from the immediate memory implies a faulty grasp of the principle of gradation. Let us give our pupils ample opportunities, on an appropriate number of occasions, of reproducing matter heard a few moments previously; this will strengthen their associations and when later on we appeal to their prolonged memory, the results will be satisfactory.

(*e*) *Chorus-work before Individual Work.* Before we call on an individual pupil to articulate a sound or a succession of sounds, let the work be done in chorus on two or more different occasions. For an individual to have to submit his tentative efforts to the criticism and perhaps laughter of his fellow pupils is not conducive to good results. Let the individual pupils test their articulation in company with others, and when by so doing they have gained a certain mastery of what they have to repeat and have thereby gained a certain degree of confidence, let them proceed to reproduce singly what they have previously phonated together.

(*f*) *Drill-work before Free Work*. This is perhaps the most important of the precepts to be observed in connexion with gradation. The forms of exercise to which the general term *drill-work* may be applied are many and varied. Some of them are calculated to train the student in perceiving and discriminating the sounds of which the language is composed; others are articulated exercises; there are also special forms of drill-work which aim at securing fluency and accuracy in producing successions of syllables. The question-and-answer method may be embodied in many interesting forms of drill-work; there exist also many varieties of action drill, conversion drill, translation drill, and grammar drill. All these forms are characterized by common attributes: they are all systematic, highly organized, and susceptible of infinite gradation; the work is methodical and proceeds steadily and continuously without breaks or interruptions. Most forms of drill-work have been composed and are carried out in such a way as to preclude the possibility of the student's forming bad habits. Indeed, if the work is carried out as designed the element of error should be almost entirely excluded.

Now *free work* in all its varied forms, such as free conversation, free translation, and free composition, differs greatly from drill-work, and we can all testify to the ludicrous results these forms of work yield when performed by one who has had no previous drilling. If the student has not been put through a proper course of drill-work, all his efforts at free work will be based on that most unnatural and vicious of processes— conventional translation from the mother tongue. The undrilled

French student will be speaking and writing not English as we understand the term, but anglicized French. Having formed no English language habits, he will cast all his thoughts in the French mould, and when the exact English equivalents to his French words and phrases are missing he will break down.

Free work without the essential preparation means faulty work, uncertain, and erratic work; it means the formation of nearly all the bad habits which characterize the average student and which mar his work.

CHAPTER 11

Proportion

In language-study as in any other branch of activity we must observe a sense of proportion; we must pay due attention to the various aspects of the question in order to ensure a harmonious whole. It is possible to devote too much time and effort to a given aspect or branch; this is the case when such time and effort are spent at the expense of an aspect or branch of equal or of greater importance. It is necessary, for instance, to give much attention to the understanding of the language as spoken rapidly and idiomatically by natives; but if this occupies the whole of our time we shall be able to do nothing else, and shall neither learn to speak, nor to read, nor to write. This would be an obvious violation of the principle of proportion. It is necessary to know something of the grammar of the language, but if we devote every lesson of a three years' course to the study of grammar we shall again be offending against this principle.

We tend to give too much attention to things which interest us, and too little to those things in which we are not particularly interested. Such inequality of treatment is more particularly apt to occur in these days of specialization; the intonation specialist thinks of little but intonation, and tends to think that everything else is of secondary importance; the phonetician is so keenly alive to the immense importance of ear-training and of correct articulation that he may tend to dismiss all other things as trivialities; the grammarian grinds away at declensions and conjugations regardless of the existence of such things as sounds and tones; the semantician is so intent on meanings that all has to be sacrificed to his special branch.

The most typical example of disproportionate treatment is,

of course, that afforded by the orthographist of the old school; for him language is nothing but a set of spelling rules; pronunciation for him is the interpretation of spellings; grammar is a branch of orthography, and meanings themselves are largely dependent on the way a word is spelt. In the present-day reaction against the orthographist we may expect a swing to the other extreme, and we may find schoolmasters welcoming spelling mistakes as the signs of a healthy tendency towards phoneticism.

Already the reaction against the over-use and abuse of translation exercises has resulted in an almost equally grave over-use and abuse of the 'direct' method.

There are, however, times when a seemingly undue proportion of attention should be directed to certain things, notably when we have to react against a vicious tendency. If our student is too keenly interested in orthography and oblivious to the importance of phonetics, we may be justified in excluding orthography from his programme. If he is morbidly interested in grammar and analysis, we may find it necessary to give him overdoses of semantics and unconscious assimilation in order to re-establish some sort of equilibrium. With the student who refuses to learn a word until he sees it written we must for some time make an exclusive and seemingly disproportionate use of oral work and phonetic writing.

The principle of proportion, then, does not necessarily imply *equality* of treatment nor even a fixed standard of ratios; it simply means that all the items in the whole range of subjects and aspects must receive an appropriate degree of attention, so that the student's knowledge of them may ultimately form a harmonious whole.

It is impossible to observe the principle of proportion without having in view the ultimate aim of the student. If his sole object is to become a master of colloquial expression, our sense of proportion will tell us to exclude in a very large measure the study of the conventional orthography.

The ultimate aim of most students is fourfold:

(a) To understand the language when spoken rapidly by natives.

(b) To speak the language in the manner of natives.

(c) To understand the language as written by natives (i.e. to *read* the language).

(d) To write the language in the manner of natives.

Each of these four aspects requires special methods of teaching. A method or device which will rapidly enable the student to understand the language when spoken will be inefficacious as a method for teaching him to produce a written composition. No amount of composition work, on the other hand, will teach him how to understand what is rapidly uttered by natives. If (as is freely admitted) a command of the spoken language is a great help towards acquiring command of the written, the converse is not the case; proficiency in written work does not imply progress in oral work. To pay too much or too little attention to any of these four aspects is a violation of the principle of proportion.

The principle may also be violated by paying too much or too little attention to any of the five chief branches of practical linguistics: phonetics, orthography, word-building, sentence-building, and semantics. Let us pass them in review in order to make quite sure that we understand the scope of each and have properly discriminated between them.

Phonetics teaches us how to recognize and how to make the sounds of which the language is composed; it teaches us the difference between two or more sounds which resemble each other, and between a given foreign sound and its nearest native equivalent.

Orthography (with which we may associate orthoepy) teaches us how to spell what we have already learnt by ear; it also teaches us how to pronounce what we have learnt by eye from an ordinary orthographic text.

78

Word-building (accidence and etymology) teaches us inflexions, prefixes, and suffixes, and how to use them, how to form plurals from singulars, accusatives from nominatives, finite tenses from infinitives; most of the mysteries of declension and conjugation are included under this heading; the collecting of word-families pertains to this branch.

Sentence-building (syntax and analysis) teaches us how to combine words into sentences, how to form compound tenses, phrases, and clauses; it teaches us the places of the various sentence-components, the nature and use of concord or agreement; it shows us the differences between regular and irregular sentences. When properly systematized (according to a special science to which the name of 'ergonics' has been given) this particular branch of linguistics shows us how to form the largest possible number of sentences with the fewest words.

Semantics teaches us the meaning of words, of inflexions, and of compounds; it shows us how to transform our thoughts into language, to select the most appropriate word or form, and to interpret correctly what we hear and read. It is more especially this branch which teaches us the differences in style and dialect, and enables us to distinguish the colloquial from the classical and to keep either from contaminating the other.

If we are to judge by the average teacher and the average language-course, the principle of proportion is usually violated by teaching:

(*a*) No phonetics at all.
(*b*) Too much orthography or orthoepy.
(*c*) Too much word-building.
(*d*) Too little sentence-building.
(*e*) Practically no semantics.

The principle of proportion may also be observed or violated in the selection of vocabularies and of grammatical material. To include in early lessons words or forms which are comparatively rare, archaic, and useless, while excluding some of the commonest and most useful items of language-material, is an offence not only against the principle of gradation but also against the principle of proportion. Too little attention also is usually paid to ensuring a just proportion between the various parts of speech. There is a fairly well-defined series of laws which determine the relative number of nouns, verbs, and adjectives occurring in a given vocabulary radius, and with the growing attention which is being given to this sort of statistical work these laws are standing out more clearly and are coming to be better understood. We have also to note a regrettable tendency to give preference in vocabularies to words of special utility (such as names of plants, animals, parts of the body, tools, implements, and such-like semi-technical words) and to neglect unduly words of general utility, words which may occur in any context and which are common to any subject. This is a particularly grave case of disproportion when we consider that the bulk of any given text (probably from 80 per cent. to 90 per cent. of it) is made up of these general words.

Proportion must be observed in determining the respective quantities of drill-work and free work, of translation-work and 'direct work', of intensive reading and extensive reading, of chorus-work and individual work needed; throughout the whole range of the subject there are possibilities of good or of bad proportion. It is for the teacher or for the designer of language-courses to see that the principle is reasonably well observed.

12

Concreteness

Such expressions as *for instance, for example,* or *here is a case in point* are fairly common in our speech. Whenever we hear somebody explaining something we may be certain that one of these expressions will occur not once but many times. When we ourselves set out to explain anything we may be quite sure that in a very few moments we shall use one of the expressions in question, and indeed our certainty is justified in almost every case. The reason for using such phrases is quite clear; every time we do so it is because we feel instinctively that we have just made a statement which is not sufficiently explicit; we are more or less aware that we have expressed something in terms rather too abstract, and we wish to reduce our statement to more concrete terms; we feel the necessity for *concreteness.* There is a similar reason for using such expressions as *in other terms, in other words,* or *that is to say.* We feel in these cases that an explanation just given is wanting in lucidity, and we add a supplementary explanation in order to make our point more concrete.

The substance of the principle of concreteness is contained in the maxim, 'Example is better than precept'; we intuitively know this to be true, and our own experience confirms our judgment; we remember on how many occasions a few typical examples have been of greater help to our understanding than the best-worded definitions or the most detailed descriptions. Psychologists confirm us in our impression and assure us that it is correct; indeed, one of the fundamental principles of the psychology of study is that we must work from the concrete to the abstract.

Let us take a concrete example to serve as an illustration.

One of the things we have to teach the French student of English is that anterior duration is expressed in English by the use of the perfect tenses (if possible in their progressive form) and not by the use of the ordinary non-perfect tenses as in French, and that *depuis* or its equivalent is not merely *since*. The whole point can be expressed more or less abstractly by the following formula:

French		English
Non-perfect tense + *depuis* + measure of duration *or* Il y + (non-perfect tense of *avoir*) + measure of duration + *que* + non-perfect tense	=	Corresponding perfect (progressive) tense + (*for*) + measure of duration.
Non-perfect tense + *depuis* + term signifying initial moment of duration	=	Corresponding perfect (progressive) tense + *since* + term signifying initial moment of duration.

Now this is a very concise formula and probably covers the whole of the ground. But it is expressed in such abstract terms that we cannot expect the average student to grasp it, still less to apply it in his speech. We can concretize it by furnishing one or two typical examples. We can say: 'Look at the clock, it is just half-past twelve—we started this lesson at twelve, didn't we? Well, it means that we have been working since twelve o'clock; we have been working for half an hour. How long have we been working? For half an hour. Since when have we been working? Since twelve o'clock. Repeat that after me. Repeat it again. Now just note that we say *We have been working*, not *We work* or *We are working*. Now, then, how do you say *Nous travaillons depuis midi*? And *Nous travaillons depuis une demi-heure*? Note that *nous sommes* sometimes becomes *we have been*.'

That would be a fairly concrete (but not ideally concrete) way of teaching the point in question. The average student would grasp the point, and the conscientious student would probably observe it and incorporate it into his usage.

But the principle of concreteness goes beyond this; it does not merely state that examples of every rule should be given, it specifies various degrees and various kinds of concreteness. An example in itself is more concrete than a rule, but one example may be more concrete than another; let us therefore choose the more concrete examples, that is to say, those which will create the strongest semantic associations. Concreteness will be the chief determining factor in the choice of the early vocabularies; it will tend to make us give a preference to words and compounds lending themselves to 'direct' work. It will not, however, be the sole factor, for if we decided to make an exclusive use of such words it would be at the expense of the principle of proportion.

Here is another example of what is implied by concreteness. It often occurs that a student will learn how to construct a sentence—indeed, he may even memorize it—and yet fail to realize that it is a real living sentence, an integral part of his linguistic repertory ready for immediate use. He may have learnt the construction *Would you mind ——ing* and be able to translate it backwards and forwards and invariably to quote it in his list of compounds requiring the use of the *ing*-form, and yet, instead of using it in actual practice, may replace it by *Would you be so kind as to* or some such stilted equivalent. In such cases we may be sure that the principle of concreteness has not been sufficiently observed.

The 'direct methodists' of the more extreme type interpret concreteness in a curious way, and identify it with the non-translation principle and with the principle of the exclusion of the mother tongue as a vehicular language. They tend to think that by keeping English out of the French lesson, the teacher causes French to be acquired concretely. In certain cases this is true, but there are probably far more contrary cases.

In the example relating to the expression of anterior duration the concreteness consists very largely in pointing out the

D

difference of usage in the two languages. In order to make the construction *Would you mind* perfectly concrete to a Frenchman, we must insist on its semantic equivalent to his *Est-ce que ça ne vous ferait rien de*. One of the things we must do to concretize the difference between *I did so, So I did,* and *So did I,* is to furnish the student with his respective native equivalents.

There are four ways and four ways only of furnishing a student with the meaning of given foreign units:

(1) *By immediate association*, as when we point to the object or a picture of the object designated by a noun or pronoun, when we perform the action designated by a verb, when we point to a real example of the quality designated by an adjective, or when we demonstrate in similar ways that which is designated by a preposition of place or certain categories of adverbs.

(2) *By translation*, as when we give the nearest native equivalent or equivalents of the foreign unit.

(3) *By definition*, as when we give a synonym or paraphrase of the word or word-group or a description of that which is designated by it.

(4) *By context*, as when we embody the unit in sentences which will make its meaning clear (e.g. January is the *first* month of the year; London is the *capital* of England).

These four methods or modes of 'semanticizing' a unit are here given in order of what are generally their relative degrees of concreteness. There may, however, be some cases in which translation will be more concrete than immediate association. Translation is not in itself necessarily 'indirect' (or 'inconcrete', as we should prefer to express it); it may be relatively indirect when compared with good examples of immediate association, but it is undoubtedly more 'direct' than a cumbrous or vague definition, or an obscure context.

The following precepts may serve as concrete examples of the way we can carry the principles of concreteness into practice:

84

(1) Let the example precede or even replace the rule. A well-chosen example or set of examples may so completely embody the rule that the rule itself will be superfluous.

(2) Give *many* examples to each important rule. We have noted that the suggested treatment of the problem of anterior duration was not an ideal one. In order to make it ideal we should have taken a second example (e.g. *How long have you been learning English?*) and still more examples (e.g. *How long have you been in this room?—been living in England?—been living at your present address? Have you been sitting here since twelve o'clock or since a quarter past twelve? How long has France been a republic?*). Too often the teacher imagines that one example constitutes a complete exposition of a given point: whereas in reality it is by finding (consciously or unconsciously) the common element in many examples that we come to grasp the usage exemplified.

(3) When teaching or alluding to the peculiarities connected with nouns, choose as examples the nouns which are the names of various objects actually in the room, and in each case point to or handle the object in question. Handling pencils, pens, and books while talking about them very much facilitates the grasping of principles of declension.

(4) When teaching or alluding to the peculiarities connected with verbal forms, choose as examples verbs such as *take, put, see, go, come, sit, stand,* etc.—that is to say, verbs that can be 'acted'. Present, past, and future tenses are much more easily distinguished and retained if the teacher illustrates them by actions. (*In a moment I shall take the book—Je prendrai le livre. J'ouvrirai le livre—J'ouvre le livre—J'ai ouvert le livre.*) If a Frenchman cannot grasp the difference between *to go in* and *to come in,* it is because the explanations given to him are lacking in concreteness.

(5) When teaching or alluding to the peculiarities connected with adjectives, choose as examples such words as *black, white, large, small, round, square,* etc., and avoid the traditional *good, bad, beautiful, idle, diligent,* etc.

(6) When teaching or alluding to the peculiarities and semantic values of prepositions choose as far as possible prepositions such as *in, on, under, over, in front of, behind, beside,* etc. Useful work in this connexion can be done with a match and a matchbox (*in the box, on the box, under the box,* etc.).

(7) Choose as many real examples as possible, examples suggested by present and actual conditions. Do not teach the mechanism of direct and indirect objects by allusions to imaginary farmers giving imaginary oats to imaginary horses, but give books, pencils, and pens to the students and make them give them to you, and then talk to them about what you are doing. Do not illustrate the active and passive voices by reference to men beating boys and boys being beaten, but speak about writing words and words being written or about speaking English and English being spoken.

(8) In as many cases as possible cause the student to make active use of any form he has just learnt. When you have taught him to say *I don't understand* give him an opportunity of using the sentence. If you teach him to say *It's time to stop* see that he duly makes use of the expression at the end of the lesson.

(9) Encourage gestures, even in the case of English students. In the earlier stages they should shake their heads when uttering a negative sentence, raise their eyebrows when using an interrogative form, and use other appropriate gestures for such words as *here, there, me, that, these,* etc.

In short, observe the principle of concreteness by using examples, many examples, cumulative examples, real examples, and examples embodying the personal interest.

CHAPTER 13

Interest

We have laid great stress on the necessity for drill-like work, for mechanical work, for exercises calculated to secure automatism, for habit-forming types of work. It has even seemed at times that we take a malicious pleasure in pillorying and condemning precisely those forms of work which are generally the most attractive to the average student. 'The writer of this book', some may say, 'takes a savage delight in reproving teacher and student whenever they contemplate work of an interesting nature, heads them off whenever they approach anything resembling intellectual work, and turns them into channels of routine and repetition. He positively gloats over words like "automaticity", "passivity", "mechanism", or "unconscious assimilation", and apparently glories in the theory that language-learning like life itself should be "one demd horrid grind".'

We readily plead guilty to a firm insistence on habit-forming exercises and drills, but continue to urge in mitigation that the practical study of a language, the mastery of any form of actual speech, is a habit-forming process and little else. We must have the courage and honesty to face facts as we find them: a language cannot be mastered by learning interesting things about that language, but only by assimilating the material of which that language is made up.

But our attitude, far from being a pessimistic one, is positively optimistic. We are prepared to deny most emphatically that good drill-work *is* dull and uninteresting, and if some teachers make it so it is our duty to tell them not to. Those who have seen the sort of lessons that embody the forms of teaching which result from the rigid observance of these principles all testify

THE PRINCIPLES OF LANGUAGE-STUDY

that they are 'live' lessons (to use the term they most generally employ), that the students are keen and the teachers enthusiastic.

It is only too evident that every lesson must be made as interesting as is compatible with pedagogic soundness. Few people learn anything well unless they are interested in what they are learning. Hope of reward and fear of punishment are certainly stimuli to work, but very poor stimuli compared with that represented by interest. If the method is the machinery of language-study (or any other study for the matter of that) then interest is the motive power. Be the clock ever so well and ingeniously constructed, it will not go without some sort of mainspring; be the method ever so efficient as a method, it will not work unless the student is interested. All these statements are of course truisms and are accepted as axiomatic; the trouble comes when we discuss the means by which interest can be induced and maintained, for we are not all in agreement on this point.

There is, too, the question of intrinsic and extrinsic interest; the subject may be interesting in itself or it may derive an artificial sort of interest from some attendant circumstance, such as the hope of reward and fear of non-success and all that that may imply.

But a point arises at the outset which deserves our attention. A fallacy exists in connexion with interest, a fallacy which is the cause of much error and of much bad teaching. This fallacy when reduced to the absurd consists in saying, 'We can make a subject of study interesting by changing the subject of study.' Now obviously it is absurd to say that we can make the study of French interesting by teaching geometry in its stead, or that we can make arithmetic interesting by replacing the arithmetic lesson by a history lesson. And yet this is the sort of thing that frequently does take place in some form or other.

It is necessary that the student shall learn how to understand spoken French, spoken English, or spoken Pekingese; it is assumed that the necessary phonetic and oral repetition work will be uninteresting, so we change the subject and teach the student to *read* French, English, or Mandarin Chinese, or to analyse these languages or to construct sentences in them by synthesis. Now reading and analysis and synthesis may to some people be more interesting than ear-training and oral memorizing, but whether this is the case or not it is certainly beyond the point. If we wish to learn to read, let us read; if we wish to do analytic and synthetic work, let us analyse and synthesize; but if the object of our study happens to be the command of the *spoken* language, it is no use to amuse ourselves by doing work which does not further our aim.

'Parrot-work is so monotonous, uninspiring, and uninteresting: let us rather translate the work of some author into our mother tongue.' 'I don't find the study of the colloquial language elevating: I prefer to work at the classical.' Very well, we will not quarrel about tastes, but we will ask you to make it quite clear what you are setting out to learn and what your object really is; when we have ascertained that, we will see how we can make your path an easy and pleasant one. A journey to London may or may not be an interesting one, but if your object is to get to London it is no use taking a ticket to the Isle of Wight or to the Highlands of Scotland, however interesting such journeys may be.

The general tendency among educationalists today is towards interesting methods, methods involving the intelligent use of the intelligence, methods which develop the reasoning capacities, methods which form the judgment, which proceed from the trivial, familiar, and known towards the more profound, unfamiliar, and unknown. Geography is no longer a process of learning lists of place-names by heart, history is no longer represented as a catalogue of dates, arithmetic is taught by playing with cubes, chemistry is presented as a series of experiments in the laboratory, botany and geology are studied in the field. The old cramming process is being replaced by the method of discovery; the teacher furnishes the documents and the students discover the rules; the teacher suggests the problems and the pupils set their wits to work and find out the solutions. All of which is very interesting and, on the whole, very good.

There is, however, this danger: these interesting and mind-developing methods do not tend towards automatism and habit-formation; they are, indeed, not intended to foster any form of mechanical command.

Proficiency in shorthand cannot be gained by any method of discovery, and the capacity for doing good and rapid work on a typewriter is not attained by the heuristic method. Mathematics is a science, but the absolute mastery of the multiplication table is an art and cannot be gained by the exclusive practice of playing with cubes.

'The memorizing of the multiplication table is a wearisome grind; let us therefore make it interesting by teaching in its place the theory of numeration!' 'Practising scales on the piano is monotonous and inartistic; let us therefore abolish such finger-gymnastics and replace all such work by the theory of harmony!' 'Learning sentences by heart and performing these drills are so tedious; let us therefore reject these forms of work, and replace them by analysing a text or by trying our hand at literary composition!'

Now, as we have seen and proved to our satisfaction, language-learning is essentially a habit-forming process, is an *art* and not a *science*, and if we insist on considering as a science what is an art we are confusing the issues and creating a breeding-ground for all sorts of fallacies. Linguistics is a science, language-teaching is largely a science, but the practical study of languages is not; let us remember this primordial fact while we are endeavouring to make our subjects inter-esting.

What are the chief things making for interest? We suggest six rational and reasonable factors calculated to produce interest if not enthusiasm without any detriment to any of the eight other fundamental principles, viz.:

(1) The elimination of bewilderment.
(2) The sense of progress achieved.
(3) Competition.
(4) Game-like exercises.
(5) The right relation between teacher and student.
(6) Variety.

(1) *The Elimination of Bewilderment.* 'I can't make out what it's all about! What on earth is the teacher driving at? I don't understand these new terms nor the use of them. What is it all for? What good is it going to do me? I do hate this lesson!'

Have you ever heard comments of this sort? Have you ever made them yourself? The attitude of one making such comments (either openly or inwardly) is not a hopeful one; it gives no promise of successful work; it shows that interest is entirely lacking. What is the cause of this attitude, and how can we change it? Is it because the subject is too difficult? No, surely not, for some of the most difficult subjects may be most fascinating, even for the average student; difficulty often adds to the attractiveness of work and may even induce interest. Difficulty is not necessarily an unfavourable factor. But bewilderment invariably is!

There is an immense difference between difficult work and bewildering work; of difficulties there must necessarily be many, but of bewilderment there should be none.

New methods often bewilder those who have become used to the old ones; unfamiliar grammatical systems are bewildering to those who think that one system of grammar is common to all the languages of the world. It is disconcerting to face the fact that languages have classical and colloquial grammars existing side by side, which grammars are mutually exclusive in many respects; it is more especially bewildering to those who have never made any study of colloquial language. Easy things and easy systems are more bewildering than difficult ones if one has already become more or less familiar with the difficult system. To those who have wrestled for years with difficult and tangled orthographies a phonetic system of writing, the acme of ease and simplicity, may appear bewilderingly difficult. A good deal of bewilderment may be ascribed to prejudice or to preconceived notions concerning the nature of language; this is why (other things being equal) children are generally less bewildered than adults when learning how to use the spoken form of language; they have fewer prejudices or even none at all.

There are two ways of eliminating bewilderment. One is to give in the clearest possible way certain fundamental explanations whenever there appears to be confusion in the mind of the student; the other is to see that the programme is properly graded. Once the student grasps the scope of the particular problem or series of problems, and once the programme is reasonably well graded, there will be no more bewilderment and there will be no more puzzled learners.

We might perhaps add here that there are times, strangely enough, when the teacher finds it necessary to induce a temporary bewilderment. Categoric and unconventional devices have occasionally to be adopted in order to break certain undesirable associations; 'mystery words' and 'mystery sentences' often play a useful part in destroying false associations and vicious linguistic habits. But these intentionally created mysteries, puzzling for the time being, are not of the same order as those hopeless and perpetual mysteries which are the cause of so much discouragement and discomfiture.

It is a subject of debate whether we ought to use explanations at all for the purpose of teaching anyone to use a language. Some maintain that we should no more explain a point of theory to a schoolchild or an adult than we should to a child of eighteen months. The young child, it is said, learns to speak the language which he hears around him by dint of sheer imitation; he learns no theory and would understand on explanations; why therefore should we explain at all?

We would suggest that the chief function of explanations is to prevent bewilderment. It may or may not be useful for a school-child or an adult to know why certain things are so, why French nouns are either masculine or feminine, why it is sometimes *avoir* and sometimes *être*, why we do not say in English *he comesn't*, why we do not say *I had better to go*, and why certain French conjunctions require the use of the subjunctive. Appropriate explanations may induce a more rapid rate of progress or they may not (probably in the long run generally not), but they certainly do have the effect of satisfying that instinctive curiosity which, if unappeased, will induce bewilderment and so cause the student to lose interest.

We might add (although this is not pertinent to the subject under discussion) that in the case of a 'corrective course' simple and rational explanations should form an essential part of the treatment.

With regard to the second manner of eliminating the factor of bewilderment, viz. the proper grading of the course, we would refer the reader to the chapter dealing specifically with this subject.

(2) *The Sense of Progress Achieved.* All work becomes more interesting when we are conscious that we have made and are making progress in that work. That sense of discouragement which is so inimical to interest arises when, in spite of our efforts, we seem to be no nearer to our goal. Statistics compiled by those who have made a special study of the psychology of learning show us that periods frequently occur in which there is no apparent progress and during which, as a necessary consequence, the interest of the student diminishes. It is generally during such periods (technically called *plateaux*) that the adult student gives up his study as a bad job and retires from the contest.

The curse of such *plateaux* would appear to be a defective

system of gradation; the student has over-reached himself and has temporarily absorbed more material than he can retain permanently; he has worked too fast for his habit-forming capacities and has to mark time until the previously acquired material has been properly assimilated.

Novelty always gives a certain amount of interest to a new subject, and during the first period students often gain the idea that they are making more progress than is warranted by the facts; when the novelty wears off the reaction occurs, and a period of depression follows.

In order, therefore, to make it possible for the student always to feel he is making progress, and thus to maintain interest and zest, it is necessary to see that the course is properly graded, that the repetitions are kept up regularly and systematically, and that the rate of progression is consistently increased.

(3) *Competition*. The spirit of emulation gives zest to a study. The fear of being outdistanced by one's fellow students or rivals, the satisfaction of gaining ground on them, and the hope of becoming or remaining the best student in the class is a stimulus not to be despised. This is really one of the chief *raisons d'être* for examinations, tests, and registers of progress.

(4) *Game-like Exercises*. In the case of young students a considerable amount of interest can be induced by making certain forms of exercise so resemble games that the pupils do not quite know whether they are playing or working. Games of skill such as chess are almost indistinguishable from many subjects of scholastic study, and many types of puzzles and problem-games are practically identical with mathematical problems. The only danger here is that language-games may not further the student sufficiently in the habit-forming process; some types certainly will not; indeed, we can imagine types of exercise-games which would tend to inhibit it. If, however, the necessity for habit-forming is constantly present to the teacher's mind, it is permissible to introduce at appropriate moments forms of exercise such as 'action drill', 'living grammar', or

'sorting exercises', possessing real educative value and an interest-giving value at the same time.

(5) *The Relation between Teacher and Student.* 'No, I don't take French lessons now. Monsieur Untel used to be my teacher, but he went away, and I didn't much like the man who took his place, and so I lost interest and stopped. The new man was all right in his way, but it wasn't at all the same thing as with M. Untel; he didn't have the same way of giving the lessons, and somehow or other I didn't seem to get on with him.'

'I like the French lesson; M. Untel makes it so interesting; he's got a nice way of explaining things, and we are never afraid of asking him questions. He doesn't laugh at you if you say something that sounds silly; he understands what you're trying to drive at, and always knows what the trouble is. I didn't use to like French lessons at all. We had another master then; he always seemed to be telling you things that you didn't feel you wanted to know, and yet when you did want to know something he never understood what it was you wanted to know.'

These expressions of opinion (written in colloquial English) give us a good idea of why two students (one an adult and the other a schoolchild) are interested in learning French when M. Untel gives the lesson.

(6) *Variety.* A monotonous type of drill-work is performed during an entire lesson. In the next lesson a second and different type of monotonous drill-work is performed. The third lesson is devoted to a third type of drill-work. A fourth lesson consists of sixty minutes of another sort of grind. A fifth and a sixth lesson are similarly devoted to two other sorts of mechanical work. The net result is six dull and monotonous lessons.

Another case. Six lessons are given. Each lesson is divided into six periods of ten minutes. Each period is devoted to a different type of mechanical work or drill-work. The net result is six moderately interesting lessons.

Not that any lesson should consist exclusively of drill-work or mechanical work; there is a place in every lesson for listening

95

to the living language in actual use; there is a place in every lesson for interesting explanations and for the factor of human interest, for the use of devices which usually engage the keenest attention of the students. If, however, there are forms of work which generally appear less popular or less vivacious, if the repeating of word-lists and the reciting of groups of sentences do tend towards dullness, then we can compensate for this temporary lack of vivacity by introducing an extra dose of variety.

A change of work is in itself a factor of interest even if the work should not be particularly interesting; variety will relieve any tedium which may possibly be associated with mechanical work. Let us suppose that on one or more occasions we do find it necessary for some particular purpose to introduce an unpopular form of exercise; we can sandwich that exercise between two popular forms of work, and the evil ten minutes will pass unnoticed.

This point will be treated incidentally when we come to examine principle 9 (the multiple line of approach); we shall see what bearing this theory has on the question of variety and the interest engendered thereby.

CHAPTER 14

A rational order of progression

One of the greatest differences between the old-fashioned manner of teaching languages and the new manner towards which we are feeling our way is a difference in what we call 'order of progression'. This term and the principle which is involved therein cannot, at the present stage of our knowledge, be defined in very categoric terms; its connotation is somewhat loose, for it may be applied to the general programme of study and also to any particular item of study. In some ways the principle seems to have a close connexion with gradation, and yet on the whole it appears to cover other ground, for we can imagine entirely different orders of progression, and each may be well or badly graded.

Under this particular heading we have to consider the order in which the various aspects and branches of a language may be dealt with. We may conceivably work from the written to the spoken or *vice versa*; we may start with systematic ear-training and articulation exercises or leave these to a later stage; we may advise or we may reject the use of a phonetic alphabet; we may teach or we may leave intonation; we may proceed from the word towards the sentence or we may take the sentence as our starting-point; we may exclude irregularities during the early stages or we may include them; we may insist on a slow and distinct pronunciation at the outset and leave abbreviations and shortened forms to a later stage. In all these matters, and in other cases as well, we have to consider very seriously two alternatives; we have to weigh the respective advantages and disadvantages, remembering always that our object is to secure rapid but permanent progress. Each of the pairs of alternatives enumerated above has been and still is the subject of discussion and controversy; there is much to be said on both sides, and an argument in favour of the one side may seem conclusive—until we have heard the argument for the other. Let us examine each of the points we have mentioned and place the opposing views in parallel columns; for the sake of convenience we will in each case place the arguments of the older school on the left-hand side and the modern answer on the right.

Written or spoken first?

The most stable form of speech is written speech; it does not vary from one person to another or from one region to another as spoken language always does. In the written form we find the essence of a language and its treasure-house. Spoken language is a faint and attenuated counterpart, generally more or less debased and altered by slang, dialect, and slovenly habits of utterance.	The only true form of speech is spoken speech; it constitutes the living language itself. All languages were spoken long before they were written. Orthographies are comparatively recent inventions, and have no more claim to being the essence of language than shorthand. The written aspect of language is artificial; the spoken aspect alone is pursuing the normal course of evolution, and is always freeing itself from archaic and useless encumbrances. The spoken language is a token of life, for dead languages are those which exist but in written form.
An unwritten language is almost a contradiction in terms, for a language without a literature is but a barbarous jargon, primitive in its structure, weak in vocabulary and in means of expression.	The facts are all wrong. Most, if not all, unwritten languages so far investigated prove to be of a remarkable richness. The Bantu group, to quote one example, has an inflexional system rivalling and excelling those of Latin and Greek, and possesses wonderfully rich syntactical and semantic systems.
When a child goes to school, he starts learning his language on its written basis. He starts at the A B C.	In the meantime he has already become an expert user of the spoken language, including the complete phonetic system unconsidered in written speech and a most complex and beautiful system of intonation unknown to orthographies.

Grammar only exists in written language.

If the grammar of the written language only exists in the written language, the grammar of the spoken language only exists in the spoken language.

It is easier to learn a written word than a spoken word, for the written word remains before the eyes, whereas the spoken word is intangible and evanescent.

Consequently if we learn the written word we are unable to understand what is said to us and to express ourselves orally.

It is easy to convert eye-knowledge into ear-knowledge. Once we know how a word is written we easily learn how to pronounce it.

The facts are all wrong again. The most difficult thing in language-study is to convert eye-knowledge into ear-knowledge. Once we know how a word is pronounced we can recognize and reproduce its written form with the greatest ease.

Shall we start with systematic ear-training and articulation exercises?

No. Both are of doubtful value under the best of conditions. The majority of students manage eventually to understand and to make themselves understood without such adventitious and fanciful aids.

Certainly. Unless the teaching rests on this foundation all the subsequent work will be distorted and false.

The young child does not have to undergo such processes when learning his native tongue, and yet he succeeds in hearing and in articulating correctly.

The young child at the cradle age does little else than go through a course of such exercises. He listens and imitates, at first imperfectly, but later with great expertness, recognizing and reproducing isolated sounds and complex combinations of these.

Such exercises are extremely monotonous and dull; they are likely to kill interest and to cause the students to dislike the whole process of language-learning.

Such exercises are always found extremely interesting, and tend to constitute an additional attraction to the study of the language.

Few language-teachers know how to make the foreign sound correctly, and therefore few can give such exercises without causing the students to acquire bad habits.

No teacher should be allowed to do language-work who is not proficient in the sounds of the foreign language, for those who are incapable of making the sounds cannot be good language-teachers.

It is useless to attempt to teach systematically the sounds of the language, seeing that these vary from one region to another and from one person to another.

Any form of normal speech will serve as a model, provided that the speech is that of educated natives. In the absence of any model at all, the student will speak the foreign language with the sounds of his mother tongue!

Shall we admit or reject the use of phonetic transcription?

Reject it certainly, for various reasons.

Accept it certainly for various reasons.

It is extremely difficult; those who have been learning languages for years, even languages with strange alphabets, find phonetic symbols so puzzling that they are forced to discontinue their efforts.

It is extremely easy; young children learn to use it readily and accurately. Those who experience any difficulty are those who are unable or unwilling to form new habits. A language is such a difficult thing that we must utilize every means of making our work easier.

It would take weeks or even months to learn the strange and unnatural symbols.

The half a dozen strange symbols usually required in addition to those of the ordinary alphabet can usually be learnt at sight without any special practice. Even a strange 'orthographic alphabet' such as the Russian one can be mastered in a few days.

The whole proceeding is an unnatural one, contrary to all the laws of language.

All writing is an unnatural process in the sense that it is not performed by instinct, but has to be learnt as an art. Of all systems of writing, however, the phonetic system is the one most in accordance with logic and natural law.

It is trying to the eyes.

Most phonetic alphabets are clearer than those used in German and Russian, for instance.

It is a waste of valuable time to learn an artificial alphabet.

The learning of a perfectly natural alphabet is in itself of educative value; it inculcates the idea of phonetic writing and serves once for all as an essential preparation for the study of any number of foreign languages.

It is evident that the use of a phonetic alphabet will make havoc of the ordinary spelling to be learnt subsequently.

It has been ascertained experimentally that those who have been taught to read and to write a language phonetically become quite as efficient spellers as those not so trained. In many cases the phonetically trained student becomes the better speller.

To learn phonetic writing means learning two languages instead of one.

In all cases where the traditional orthography is not in agreement with the native pronunciation the student is necessarily forced to learn the two things. The use of a phonetic alphabet is the only way to perform this double work rapidly, rationally, and with the minimum of confusion.

Phonetic texts always give slovenly and incorrect manners of pronouncing words.

Authors of phonetic texts always strive to give an accurate rendering of the language as really and effectively spoken by educated natives; they rarely attempt to teach forms that have no existence in the language as actually used in ordinary speech.

Should we teach intonation in the early stages?

No. It is a fancy subject of little or no importance and certainly forms no integral part of language-study.

Yes. It is a subject of great importance and forms an integral part of language-study. In many languages speech without the correct tones is only half intelligible; in Chinese and other languages it is perfectly unintelligible.

In any case it can be left to the very final stage of the programme.

If it is not taught in the very earliest stage correct intonation will be very difficult to acquire. Language-study is a habit-forming process, and the habit of speaking with wrong tones is a bad habit.

Word or sentence first?

The word is the unit of language.	Whatever the unit of language is, it is not the word.
Words are definite entities and constitute the component parts of sentences.	Sentences may be reduced to component parts; sometimes these are words, but quite as often they are word-groups (such as compounds and phrases) or units less than words (such as affixes).
The word, not the sentence, is the basis of translation. Since a word has a definite meaning and conveys a definite idea it is easy to find the foreign equivalent.	A sentence has generally, if not always, a definite foreign equivalent. A word is so unstable that it may entirely change its meaning when used with other words.
It is easy to memorize words and difficult to memorize sentences.	It is as easy to memorize a six-word sentence as six words.
We speak in words.	We express our thoughts in sentences.
If we learn a few dozen words we can build up thousands of sentences from these by the synthetic process.	If we learn a few dozen sentences we can construct thousands of others from these by by disintegration and substitution, and, what is more, we can recognize them and use them even in rapid speech.
Words are the basis of grammar.	Sentences are the basis of syntax.
The collection of word-families is a valuable way of enriching one's vocabulary.	The enriching of one's vocabulary should be left to a comparatively late stage in the study of language, especially in the study of most derivatives and compounds.
Words constitute the 'primary matter' (i.e. matter to be memorized integrally without analysis or synthesis). Sentences constitute the 'secondary matter' (i.e. matter to be derived synthetically from primary matter).	It is precisely because sentences are so rarely considered as 'memorized matter' that so few people manage to understand the foreign language when spoken or to express themselves correctly in it.

Take care of the words and the sentences will take care of themselves.

Take care of the sentences and the words will take care of themselves.

Should irregularities be included or excluded during the earlier stages?

The regular is easy, the irregular is difficult; in the interest of gradation let us therefore exclude temporarily the irregular.

Irregular forms are generally more used and more useful than regular ones; in the interest of gradation let us therefore include all necessary irregularities even in the earlier stages.

Irregular forms make it difficult to formulate precise rules.

Rules with numerous exceptions are not worth formulating at all.

The normal and logical should precede the normal and illogical.

Then, as natural languages are full of abnormalities and bad logic, let the student start with an artificial language!

Immediate fluency or gradual fluency?

It is easy to pronounce a sentence slowly and distinctly; difficult to pronounce it rapidly and fluently.

It is just as easy to pronounce a sentence rapidly and fluently as to pronounce it slowly; it is even easier in some cases. The converse is only true when we are constructing our sentences synthetically, word by word, but this is not a sound process.

It is more correct to articulate clearly and deliberately.

To articulate more clearly and deliberately than the average educated native is a mark of inaccuracy, for, as Dr. Cummings says, 'fluency is an integral part of accuracy'.

'Shortened forms', such as *don't* or *I'm* should never be taught. The student, alas! will only too soon pick up these undesirable vulgarisms. Don't hasten the process.

All 'shortened forms' which are invariably used in normal speech by educated natives (e.g. *don't*, *I'm*) should be taught to the exclusion of the longer form. The student, alas! will only too soon acquire the habit of using pedanticisms. Let us not hasten the process.

It is always easy, too easy, to transform clear and incisive speech into a blurred and slovenly style of speaking.

It is almost impossible, in the case of foreign students, to convert an over-distinct and halting speech into a smooth, harmonious style of utterance with the proper cadence and rhythm. It is for this reason that when a foreigner wishes to say *Sunday, two to two,* or *four for four,* we so frequently understand *some day,* 2, 2, 2, or 4, 4, 4.

A vowel or even a consonant may perhaps disappear when we are speaking very rapidly or very carelessly. When, however, we are deliberately teaching a word, we should give the most perfect model and employ the most sonorous forms.

The maintenance of such syllables in ordinary rapid speech is one of the characteristics of pidgin or foreigner's speech. It is not yet sufficiently realized that the use of certain sounds is only correct in slow speech or in isolated words. If 'stayshun' is a more sonorous and correct rendering of s-t-a-t-i-o-n than 'stayshn', then 'stayshon' is still better, and 'stay-si-on' or 'stay-ti-on' better still.

Conclusion

On the basis of the foregoing considerations, we conclude that it is desirable, if not essential:

On the basis of the foregoing considerations, we conclude that it is desirable, if not essential:

(*a*) To learn to read and to write before learning to speak and to understand what is said.

(*a*) To learn to speak and to understand what is said before learning to read and to write.

(*b*) To avoid systematic ear-training and articulation exercises, at any rate in the early stages.

(*b*) To start a language-course with systematic ear-training and articulation exercises.

(*c*) To reject the use of phonetic transcription.

(*c*) To make a most extensive use of the phonetic transcription, especially in the early stages.

(*d*) To leave to a very late stage or to omit altogether the study of intonation.

(*d*) To teach intonation at a very early stage.

(*e*) To memorize words and to learn to inflect them, before memorizing and learning how to construct sentences.

(*e*) To memorize sentences and to learn how to construct them, before memorizing words and learning how to build either inflected forms or derivatives.

(*f*) To avoid irregular and idiomatic forms in the earlier stages.

(*f*) To include irregular and idiomatic forms even in the earlier stages.

(*g*) To pronounce very slowly and distinctly, leaving fluency to a later stage.

(*g*) To teach from the outset a rapid and fluent style of pronunciation, reserving more distinct utterance to a later stage.

All our experience leads us to endorse most emphatically all the statements made in the right-hand column.

Numbers of those who were formerly of the opinion expressed in the left-hand column have become and are becoming converted to the opposite view; the contrary case is practically unknown. The modernists are not arguing in the dark; they have their data and their evidence, and are perfectly well acquainted with the arguments of the ancients, whereas few of those professing the older views have ever even heard of the modernists' case, still less given it any reasonable amount of consideration.

We should note that the protagonists of each of the two schools are not invariably as sharply and as consistently divided as in the foregoing comparison. It is only natural that we should find individuals taking the modern view in the case of certain of the points quoted, and the ancient view in the other cases.

An enthusiastic adherent of the phonetic theory will not necessarily endorse the view that rapid and fluent speech should precede slow and distinct speech. One may believe in teaching sentences before words and yet be unconvinced as to the necessity for phonetics and all that that implies. Some may favour the memorizing of sentences at an early stage, but will not agree that the colloquial language should be given a more favoured place than the classical.

The two schools, however, do appear to be fairly well defined, for in the majority of cases it will most probably be found that those who favour the ancient view in any one respect will generally favour the whole of the ancient programme and regard with distrust and misgivings the order of progression generally recommended by the modernists.

Let us sum up, and set forth in parallel columns the two most widely differing orders of progression in order that we may fully realize that each is the antithesis of the other.

THE ANCIENT ORDER (based on tradition)	THE MODERN ORDER (based on psychology)
First, learn how to convert 'dictionary-words' (i.e. etymons) into 'working sentence-units' (i.e. ergons). This will be done by memorizing the rules of derivation.	*First*, become proficient in recognizing and in producing foreign sounds and tones, both isolated and in combinations.
Secondly, learn the general structure of sentences. This will be done chiefly by reading and translation exercises.	*Secondly*, memorize (without analysis or synthesis) a large number of complete sentences chosen specifically for this purpose by the teacher or by the composer of the course.
Thirdly, memorize the irregular or idiomatic phenomena of the language.	*Thirdly*, learn to build up all types of sentences (both regular and irregular) from 'working sentence-units' (i.e. ergons) chosen specifically for this purpose by the teacher or by the composer of the course.
Lastly, (if necessary) convert the 'eye-knowledge' of the language into 'ear-knowledge' by means of reading aloud and by 'conversation-lessons'.	*Lastly*, learn how to convert 'dictionary words' (i.e. etymons) into 'working sentence-units' (i.e. ergons).

An irrational order of progression is bound to entail much 'cramming', a process by which much information (valuable or valueless) is retained for a short time (generally for examination purposes), but without ensuring any permanent results except bad results.

A rational order of progression will not only rapidly secure useful and desirable results, but will also encourage the formation of the right sort of language-habits and ensure as a permanent result the capacity for using the foreign language in the fullest sense of the term.

CHAPTER **15**

The multiple line of approach

The ninth and last of the essential principles is, in reality, more than a mere principle of language-study, it is even more than a principle of study, it is almost a philosophy in itself. It seems to be a special application of a doctrine which, to many, constitutes a line of conduct, an attitude, towards most of the problems and interests of our daily existence. This attitude is fairly well designated by the term *eclectic*; this, however, is not an ideal term, seeing that, like so many others, it possesses a double connotation. Its first sense is distinctly pejorative; it suggests unoriginality, a lack of coherent system, a patchwork of other people's opinions. In its second and broader sense, so far from being a term of disparagement or reproach it implies the deliberate choice of all things which are good, a judicious and reasoned selection of all the diverse factors the sum of which may constitute a complete and homogeneous system. If, therefore, we speak here of the doctrine or attitude of eclecticism, we are obviously using the term in its second and broader connotation; used in this way it stands as the antithesis of prejudice, of faddiness, of crankiness, and of fixed ideas. Many of those who practise eclecticism call it the 'philosophy of the complete life'; whether this is or is not a philosophy in the true sense of the term, we will leave to philosophers to discuss; we will content ourselves by quoting a few maxims or aphorisms which will serve to make clear the attitude in question.

All is good which tends towards good.

The recognition and appreciation of any particular good thing does not necessarily invalidate those things which do not resemble it, nor even cause us to disparage or deprecate things which are seemingly in conflict with it.

Let us neglect nothing except futilities and things which we have proved to our satisfaction to be in themselves bad and harmful.

Two or more opposing principles, ideas, likes, operations, interests, in short any two or more conflicting tendencies, may be combined, and this combination can be effected by other means than the expedient of compromising. Lobster salad and fruit salad may be attractive to the gourmet, but no compromise between the two would be palatable.

It is not always the height of wisdom and expediency to kill too many birds with one stone.

This attitude towards life in general does indeed solve many problems and vexed questions. It constitutes a method of conciliating inconsistencies, both real and apparent. It explains how it is that one can appreciate both classical and popular music, classical and light literature, how idealism may exist side by side with a keen interest in material things. The real and the ideal, scientific precision and unscientific emotion, patriotism and internationalism, are not incompatible with each other in the 'philosophy of the complete life'.

And what has all this to do with language-study? What bearing have these fanciful or fantastical philosophical considerations on the problem of teaching or learning a language rapidly and well? The connexion is clearer than one might imagine at first sight, for each of the aphorisms quoted above may serve, if not as a definition of the ninth principle, at least as a strong suggestion of what the principle implies.

Those who have followed us, point by point, in our enumeration and analysis of the eight preceding principles may be in perfect agreement with our conclusions, but may, nevertheless, be sorely troubled as to how they are to be carried out in practice. On many points there appear to be conflicts and inconsistencies; in many cases it would appear to be exceedingly difficult, if not impossible, to observe two or more of these principles simultaneously. How is habit-forming consistent with interest? How can we combine a study of phonetics with a study of orthography? How can we combine the development of our spontaneous capacities with that of our studial capacities? How can we observe the principle of accuracy and combine it with other principles which are seemingly in conflict with it—such as the inhibition of our powers of analysis and synthesis? How are we to foster a keen appreciation of the classical or literary style of composition, and yet concentrate on the colloquial and trivial? The principles of gradation and of order of progression seem to reveal inconsistencies when they are compared with each other; there is more than a seeming inconsistency between the process of unconscious assimilation and the principle of concreteness. Translation is destructive, or is often considered so, of the power of 'thinking in the foreign language', and yet it is suggested that the student should do translation work and at the same time train himself to think in the foreign language.

These and many other problems or difficulties suggested by the careful study of the foregoing eight principles can only be solved by the thorough understanding of the spirit of eclecticism underlying this ninth principle. We have alluded to the philosophy of the complete life in order that we may better realize the significance of what we may term the complete method.

This complete method, mark you, is not a compromise between two or more antagonistic schools; it boldly incorporates what is valuable in any system or method of teaching and refuses to recognize any conflict, except the conflict between the good and the inherently bad. The complete method will embody every type of teaching except bad teaching, and every process of learning except defective learning.

The complete method (of which the multiple line of approach is the expression) is the antithesis of the special or patent method. Patent or proprietary methods very often, but not always, resemble patent medicines. We know what they are. A patent language method, like a patent medicine, claims to prevent or to cure all possible ills (linguistic or physical, as the case may be) by repeated applications of one special device or drug; both of them claim to kill innumerable birds with one stone. One is always inclined to doubt the efficiency of an instrument which is designed to perform too many distinct functions; a tool designed to serve both as a hairbrush and as a hammer is not likely either to brush or to hammer very efficiently, and our imagination refuses to picture what one vehicle could possibly afford us all the advantages of a bicycle, a motor-car, a wheelbarrow, and an express train, not to mention those of a boat or balloon. One dish, however nutritive, succulent, and satisfying, will not constitute a complete banquet.

Let us apply the principle of the multiple line of approach to the solving of a number of vexed questions, well known to all those who have read or participated in discussions and controversies on the subject of language-teaching.

Shall reading be intensive or extensive? That is to say, shall we take a text, study it line by line, referring at every moment to our dictionary and our grammar, comparing, analysing, translating, and retaining every expression that it contains? Or shall we take a large number of texts and read them rapidly and carelessly, trusting that quantity will make up for the lack of quality in our attention and the lack of intensity?

Shall we translate? We can learn much from translation; it affords us many types of interesting and valuable exercises. Or shall we ban translation? For we know that under certain conditions translation may foster and encourage more than one vicious tendency.

Shall we memorize sentences or shall we learn to construct them, both synthetically and by the substitution process?[1] Either plan seems to have its advantages and its disadvantages.

[1] See page 121 and footnote, and p. 122.

Which is better: drill-work or free work? The principle of accuracy inclines us towards the former; the principle of interest and our instinctive striving for naturalness incline us towards the latter.

Are we to study with conscious attention or with effortless attention? In the average lesson or language-course, the former alone is considered, but the young child, or the adult assimilating a language under ideal conditions, knows no other than the latter.

Shall we assimilate our language-material by reading or by listening to people? Many claim to have mastered a language rapidly and successfully by the one method, while many others ascribe their success to the fact that they have learnt exclusively by the other.

Which is the best method of retaining language-material: by repeating it aloud or by writing it? There again, we find many who are staunch adherents of either method (and consequently opponents of the other).

Active or passive work? Do we gain and retain our impressions by speaking and writing, or do we in reality acquire proficiency in the use of language by the processes of reading and listening?

Without the principle of the multiple line of approach there are only two ways of settling these and all similar questions. One is to adopt one alternative, rejecting the second; the other is to effect a working compromise between the two. Shall we read intensively or extensively? 'Read intensively', says one: 'No, read extensively', says another; and the compromiser comes along and says, 'Read neither very intensively nor very extensively'. Shall we translate or shall we banish translation? 'Translate by all means', says one; 'Banish translation', says another; and the compromiser says, 'Translate a little occasionally, but do not let the translation be particularly good'. Drill-work or free work? The compromiser suggests something between the two, mechanical enough to destroy naturalness, and free enough to encourage inaccuracy. Shall we memorize sentences, or shall we construct them? The compromiser suggests that we should aid our memory by doses of mental synthesis, in fact just enough to prevent the laws of memorizing from operating.

The principle of the multiple line of approach suggests a third and better procedure. Instead of accepting the one and rejecting the other, instead of adopting the middle course which frequently militates against the success of either extreme, this principle says: 'Adopt them both concurrently, but not in one and the same operation. At times read intensively; at others read extensively. At appropriate moments, and for specific purposes, make the fullest use of all sorts of translation work; at other moments, and for other specific purposes, banish translation entirely. At times, more especially during the early stages, let there be an abundance of drill-work; later, but not before the student is perfectly ripe for it, let us introduce free work; and then let the two types alternate. At certain moments, more especially during the early stages, let the memorizing of sentences be carried out on a most extensive scale; at other moments, as a distinctly separate operation, let us cause the student to perform exercises in constructing correct sentences himself.'

We have had occasion to note that this principle suggests the inadvisability of killing too many birds with one stone. The principle goes farther and adds to the figure of speech just quoted the two following corollaries, viz.: 'Find the right stone to kill the right bird', and 'It is often advisable to kill one bird with more than one stone.' There are many different ways of teaching a difficult sound, there are many different ways of teaching a difficult point in grammar, a curious form of construction, or of causing the student to discriminate between two things which ought not to be confused. In these and in all similar cases, there is no reason why several methods should not be used concurrently; they need not be strictly co-ordinated.

The cumulative effect of approaching the difficulty from different and independent angles will certainly secure the desired result. Superficial and rapid work on most points plus intensive and thorough work on certain essential specific points will generally ensure a well-assimilated whole. Either of these methods will tend to correct any disadvantages attached to the other and will be complementary to the other. The high degree of accuracy which results from intensive work will tend to spread by contagion to that portion of the work which must necessarily be done in a more summary fashion.

This principle, which underlies all others, leaves the door open for new devices, new methods, and improvements on the old ones. It leaves us free to welcome and to adopt all sorts of innovations, provided such innovations are likely to prove of value.

We will quote one example of what may happen when we do not sufficiently realize the importance or the scope of the ninth principle.

The teacher of French may consider that a certain amount of theory is useful and helpful; he may consider it necessary to explain all manner of things to students—how certain sounds are formed, how certain verbs are conjugated, why certain constructions must be used; he may consider it his duty to give information on hundreds of doubtful or difficult points. And he is often perfectly justified in doing so; explanations of the right sort and given at the right moment are indeed valuable.

This same teacher considers also that many opportunities should be given of hearing French spoken, in order to train his student's powers of observation and of semantic association. This also is good and reasonable; passive audition, unconscious or semi-conscious assimilation, immediate understanding and expression, are processes the value of which we have always insisted upon.

But this teacher, too anxious to kill two birds with one stone, combines the two forms of work; he says, 'I have a number of difficult things to explain, and I will explain them in French; the student will therefore have a double gain.' The student, however, unless already very considerably advanced, is not a gainer but a loser; he fails to understand the explanation, and in his efforts to do so he fails to adopt the proper receptive attitude towards the actual language material. After all, we do not learn how to write shorthand from books written exclusively in shorthand, and the book which teaches us how to use the Morse code is not printed exclusively in the Morse code. To use the foreign language for the purposes of a vehicular language under the pretext that the more the student hears of the foreign language the better he will learn, is a method which stands fully condemned when we properly realize the nature and scope of the principle we are now examining.

We may sum up this principle of the multiple line of approach fairly concisely in the following terms: Let us approach the language, or any specific point in the language, simultaneously from several distinct points of departure, by several distinct but gradually converging avenues. The observing of this principle will alone enable us to observe consistently and successfully the eight other vital principles which it has been the object of this book to set forth.

CHAPTER 16

'Memorized matter' and 'constructed matter'

Until we know more about speech-psychology and the ultimate processes of language-study, it is doubtful whether we can embody in the form of a concrete principle the subject treated in this chapter. The writer would prefer, at this stage of our knowledge, simply to submit the following considerations in the hope that future research will throw further light on the subject and render it possible to co-ordinate it with those branches of linguistic pedagogy which are more familiar to us. Indeed, when we have ascertained experimentally the exact nature of what we shall call 'memorized' and 'constructed' speech-material, it is conceivable that the whole subject will become so clarified that it will be possible to reduce to one main principle all or most of what has been said in the foregoing chapters.

Now, whenever we open our lips to speak, or whenever we set pen to paper, it is with the object of producing one or more *units of speech*. These units may be short and simple, such as: *Yes, No, Here*, or they may be word-groups, such as: *Very well, I don't know, Yes, if I can*, or they may be complete and even complicated sentences containing one or more subordinate clauses. But whatever the unit may be, long or short, simple or complex, one thing is clear: *each unit has either been memorized by the user integrally as it stands or else is composed by the user from smaller and previously memorized units*. This is a fundamental fact about speech which stands out clearly and unmistakably; it is not a fanciful supposition or an idle conjecture, it is an axiomatic truth.

Now let us term 'memorized matter' everything that we have

memorized integrally, and 'constructed matter' everything that we have not so memorized, but which we compose or build up as we go on. Can we distinguish the two things? In most cases we can. Monosyllabic words have generally (although not necessarily) been memorized as they stand; we say and understand the word *cat*, because once upon a time we had the occasion to hear the word in question and the opportunity to connect it with its meaning and to retain it. The word *cat* is included in our memorized matter. Probably most words of two or even more syllables have been acquired as memorized matter. Great numbers of compound words have also been acquired in the same way. A considerable number of word-groups and sentences are included in our memorized matter. Such sentences as *I don't know, Just come here, Pick it up, I don't want it*, are most probably memorized with most speakers.

Now consider a unit of speech such as: *I saw Henry Siddings between six and half-past at the corner of Rithington Lane.* Is it the sort of unit which we should use as a result of having memorized it integrally? An actor or reciter may indeed have occasion to do so, but apart from those whose duty or hobby it is to memorize 'lines' it is an extremely unlikely specimen of memorized matter. The writer has just composed it, and does not even know whether there exists such a surname as Siddings or a place called Rithington Lane; there are millions of chances to one that it is an entirely original sentence. Most of the things we utter or write come into the category of constructed matter; their component parts have been memorized integrally and so constitute memorized matter; but the complete units are *constructed*, they are the result of rapid and probably unconscious acts of synthesis.

This is no place for statistics, even if data were available; it must be left to investigators to ascertain the relative amount of memorized and constructed matter used by the young child in his first months or years of speech. Inquiries of this sort should afford some valuable and surprising evidence; the writer has had occasion to note that a French-speaking child of about ten was even unconscious of the composition of units such as *pomme de terre* or *quatre-vingts*, just as the average adult English person is unconscious of the composition of *fortnight* or *nevertheless*.[1] What will certainly complicate such research work is the paradoxical fact that constructed matters may become memorized by dint of frequent repetition. A further complication is added by the fact that the two types of matter may also be considered from the point of view, not of the speaker, but of the auditor.

One of the questions that concerns us at present is to ascertain what should be the right proportions of memorized and constructed matter in the initial stages of learning a foreign language.

Too large a proportion of memorized matter will render study unnecessarily tedious, for memorizing work, even under the best of conditions, is less interesting than the piecing together of known units. Too large a proportion of constructed matter, on the other hand, will certainly result in an artificial sort of speech or a pidgin form, with all its evil consequences. At the present day, as in the past, the tendency in language-study is to pay far too much attention to constructing and not nearly enough to memorizing.

What concerns us still more is to ascertain definitely by experiment what is the exact nature of those processes by which constructed matter is derived from memorized matter. We must find out what really does happen in the case of young children in the first stages of their speech-experience, and by what mental processes those persons called born linguists attain their results.

There would appear to be three distinct manners of producing constructed matter; these may be termed respectively:

[1] See *The Scientific Study and Teaching of Languages*, pp. 103–19.

(a) Grammatical construction.
(b) Ergonic construction.
(c) Conversion.

(a) Grammatical Construction

This process consists in memorizing 'dictionary words' (the infinitives of verbs, the nominative singular of nouns, the masculine nominative singular of adjectives, etc.) and of forming sentences from them (with or without the intervention of translation) by means of applying the various rules of accidence, syntax, derivation, and composition.

The following is a typical example of the process. An English student wishes to form as constructed matter the German sentence: *Ich habe mit grösstem Vergnügen seinen freundlichen Vorschlag angenommen*, from the previously memorized units *ich, haben, mit, gross, Vergnügen, sein, freundlich, Vorschlag, annehmen*. Besides having to determine (in accordance with rules of word-order) the relative position of the nine primary units, he has to perform the twelve following operations:

(1) Choose the appropriate form of the pronoun of the first person singular.
(2) Choose the appropriate tense of the verb *annehmen*.
(3) Derive the present tense first person singular form of *haben*.
(4) Determine the case governed by the preposition *mit*.
(5) Derive the superlative form of the adjective *gross*.
(6) Determine the gender of the noun *Vergnügen*.
(7) Derive the masculine dative singular form of the superlative adjective *grösst*—when not preceded by a determinative.
(8) Determine the gender of the noun *Vorschlag*.
(9) Determine the function of the same in this particular sentence.
(10) Determine the form of the possessive adjective of the

third person masculine singular when modifying a masculine accusative singular noun.

(11) Determine the form of the adjective *freundlich* when preceded by a possessive adjective and when modifying a masculine accusative noun.

(12) Derive the past participle *angenommen* from the infinitive.

It will be noticed that most of these operations require, in addition to a perfect memory of the grammatical rules (including numbers of word-lists), a fine power of logical discrimination. Needless to say, no speaker of German actually does perform any of these operations (except perhaps on very special and rare occasions), and we dismiss as a patent absurdity the supposition that the young native child constructs his matter in any such way.

(b) Ergonic Construction

In this process we work from an entirely different sort of memorized matter; instead of being merely 'dictionary words' it consists of *(a)* more or less complete sentences, and *(b)* units of speech which we may term 'ergons', i.e. 'working units' derived and inflected in advance by the teacher (or the author of the course), each ergon being thus quite ready for use.

The following is a typical example of the process:

A fairly simple sentence is memorized; let us say, *Ich kann meinen Stock heute nicht nehmen.* 'I can't take my stick today.' Appropriate groups of ergons are also memorized, such as:

A

ich, *I*

B

kann, *can*
muss, *must*
soll, *am to*
werde, *shall*
könnte, *could*
musste, *had to*

sollte, *ought to*
würde, *should*

C

meinen Stock, *my stick*
meinen Bleistift, *my pencil*
Ihren Regenschirm, *your umbrella*
den Stuhl, *the chair*
denselben, *the same*
ihn, *him, it*
sie, *her, it*
es, *it*

D

heute, *today*
morgen, *tomorrow*
heute morgen, *this morning*
morgen früh, *tomorrow morning*
um zwei Uhr, *at two o'clock*
nächsten Monat, *next month*
nächste Woche, *next week*
nächstes Jahr, *next year*

E

nicht, *not*

F

nehmen, *take*
sehen, *see*
bringen, *bring, take*
tragen, *carry, take*
suchen, *look for*
finden, *find*
bekommen, *get*

The student will then form (as constructed matter) as many of the 3,584 resultant sentences[1] as is considered

[1] See *100 English Substitution Tables*, by the author of the present book (Heffer, Cambridge). Also the series of 'Auto-Translators' (International Students' Bureau, 56 Russell Square, W.C.1).

necessary for this particular vocabulary. This will be done by means of drills and habit-forming exercises based on the following substitution table:

A	B	C	D	E	F
Ich	kann	meinen Stock	heute	nicht	nehmen
	muss	meinen Bleistift	morgen		sehen
	soll	Ihren Regenschirm	heute morgen		bringen
	werde	den Stuhl	morgen früh		tragen
	könnte	denselben	um zwei Uhr		suchen
	musste	ihn	nächsten Monat		finden
	sollte	sie	nächste Woche		bekommen
	würde	es	nächstes Jahr		

The essential difference between grammatical and ergonic construction lies in the sort of memorized matter used in either case. In grammatical construction the memorized matter consists exclusively of what we have called 'dictionary words' (a large proportion of which require modifying in some form or other before being available for use in a sentence), whereas in ergonic construction two sorts of memorized matter are required: a more or less complete sentence and a number of ergons (units of language inflected or composed in advance for the student, instead of by the student).

(c) Conversion
This process consists in memorizing a number of sentences all composed in a more or less uniform way.

When these sentences have been memorized, the student is taught by a series of appropriate drills and habit-forming exercises to convert each sentence into another form.

The following is a typical example of the process. The student memorizes the ten following sentences:

(1) *He goes to the station.*
(2) *He comes here.*
(3) *He takes it.*

(4) *He waits for it.*
(5) *He stays there.*
(6) *He writes a letter.*
(7) *He reads a book.*
(8) *He speaks French.*
(9) *He gets up.*
(10) *He's here.*[1]

He then listens to the teacher, who says:

He goes to the station . .	*He doesn't go to the station.*
He comes here . . .	*He doesn't come here.*
etc.	etc.

and after one or more repetitions performs the conversion
himself in the same way, with or without prompting by the
teacher or the book.

The teacher will then change the sentences in some other
manner, for instance:

He goes to the station . .	*Does he go to the station?*
He comes here . . .	*Does he come here?*
etc.	etc.

The student listens, and subsequently performs the same series.
On other occasions each of the ten sentences may be converted
into forms such as:

He'll go to the station, etc.
He wants to go to the station, etc.
He's going to the station, etc.
He didn't go to the station, etc.
He went to the station, etc.
He's gone to the station, etc.
It's impossible for him to go to the station, etc.
He always goes to the station, etc.

In the case of conversion the difference between memorized

[1] The inclusion of an exceptional form ('He isn't here') in a conversion table is a
useful feature in these exercises.

123

and constructed matter is not so marked as in the two synthetic operations, nor is the yield of constructed matter so great. Indeed, in extreme cases, the form into which the original sentence is to be converted will have to be learnt integrally, and so becomes in itself memorized matter. On the other hand, some forms of this type of work are practically identical with exercises based on ergonic construction, and for these two reasons it has been held that conversion is not a distinct process for forming constructed matter, but merely a modified form of ergonic work. Whether this view is justified or not is a matter more of academic than of practical interest to the language-teacher.

These then appear to be the only three processes known by which memorized matter can be developed and expanded into original composition. What we have called grammatical construction is the classical and almost universal method. What we have called ergonic construction is embodied more or less unsystematically in a number of language-courses and the more enlightened books of instruction. Conversion is also practised, but still in a sporadic and desultory fashion.

Now, some thirty years ago the reform movement started. In several different countries bands of zealous pioneers took up arms against the then prevailing system and sought to put an end to it. The reform prospered. The reformers have carried all before them, and the daring innovators of twenty or thirty years ago now enjoy the prestige that their efforts have earned for them.

What was the nature of this reform? What abuses has it swept away? And for what innovations have we to thank it? It would appear, on analysis, to have had a threefold object:

(a) To promote the rational and systematic study of pronunciation by means of phonetic theory and transcription.

(b) To promote the idea that a language is used primarily as a means of communicating thoughts.

(c) To promote the idea that foreign languages should be learned by methods approximating to those by which we learn our native tongue.

The first two objects have certainly been attained; phonetics is the order of the day, and both teachers and students have to use phonetic symbols whether they like it or not; moreover, the new generation does recognize that the deciphering and analysis of ancient texts is not the primary use of language.

The third object has not been so successfully pursued; indeed, we are still very far from learning the foreign tongue by the same processes as those by which we learnt our own. The chief reason for this failure was a bad diagnosis of the chief evils of the system hitherto employed. Many of the reformers and most of their disciples imagined 'translation' to be the root of the evil, and so translation in every shape or form was banned; there must be no bilingualism at all, and so the mother tongue must be excluded from the course, the lessons must be conducted entirely in the foreign language.

But translation and the use of the mother tongue, as it turns out, are perfectly harmless and in many cases positively beneficial; the evil lay in the exaggerated attention which had always been paid to grammatical construction; that was the dragon that the St. Georges might well have slain had not the red herring of 'translation' unfortunately been drawn across the track. As it was, the red herring was duly run down and annihilated, and the dragon still lives!

The misunderstanding was natural enough; logicians would quote it as an example of the fallacy of the False Cause. The process of grammatical construction was carried out by means of a vicious form of translation exercise, and the result was utterly bad. Two important reforms might have been effected: in the first place, the vicious form of translation might have been replaced by a beneficial form; and secondly, new and more worthy uses of translation might have been found. But the act

125

of translation itself (nay, the mere use of the mother tongue) was made the scapegoat and so paid the penalty. It is now time for a second band of reformers to attack and to destroy the original cause of unsuccessful language-study, viz. grammatical construction, or at any rate to limit it to special cases and to appropriate occasions. It is time, too, to rehabilitate in some measure the character of the comparatively innocent process of translation, and to remove the stigma attached to those who still use the mother tongue as a vehicular language, and by so doing proceed naturally enough from the known to the unknown.

These are no reactionary suggestions; they are made in the spirit of the nine essential principles treated in the previous chapters, and are not in contradiction to the urgent plea set forth in these pages for the recognition and fostering of our 'spontaneous' capacities for language-study. We can afford to ignore no necessary tool in our efforts to teach well and to produce perfect results, and translation is often a necessary tool, especially during the process of deriving constructed from memorized matter.

We suggest for the moment no tenth principle based on these considerations; we submit the problem and we more than hint at a solution. It is now time for experimental work on 'ergonic' lines, and the data to be obtained thereby will enable us to form our conclusions and to embody them among the principles of language-study.

Synopsis

1. *We possess Natural or Spontaneous Capacities for acquiring Speech*
In order to become proficient in most arts, we are assumed to study, i.e. to make conscious efforts persistently and perseveringly; we are assumed to use our intelligence. There is, however, one complex art in which all of us have become proficient without any such process and without using our intelligence consciously, viz. *the art of speech*, i.e. of using the spoken form of a language as actually used in everyday life. We are endowed by nature with capacities for assimilating speech. Each of us is a living testimony to this fact, for each of us has successfully acquired that form of our mother tongue with which we have been in contact. These capacities are not limited to the acquiring of our mother tongue, but are also available for one or more languages in addition. The young child possesses these capacities in an active state; consequently he picks up a second or a third language in the same manner as he does the first. The adult possesses these same capacities, but generally in a latent state; by disuse he has allowed them to lapse. If he wishes, he may re-educate these powers and raise them to the active state; he will then by this means become as capable as the child of assimilating foreign languages. Those adults who have maintained these powers in an active state are said to have a gift for languages.

2. *Our Studial Capacities and how to use them*
In addition to certain *spontaneous* capacities, we possess what we may term '*studial*' capacities for language-acquisition. These must be utilized when we learn how to *read* and *write* a language, and also when we wish to learn forms of language not actually used in everyday speech (i.e. the literary, oratorical, or ceremonious forms). The methods by which we utilize these capacities are generally characterized by *conscious* work (such as

127

analysis and synthesis) and by conversion, i.e. converting written into spoken (reading aloud), converting spoken into written (dictation), converting from one language into another (translation), or converting one grammatical form into another (conjugation, declension, etc.). All exercises requiring the use of the eyes and the hand are of the studial order, as are also those connected with accidence and derivation.

Most of those forms of work by which we utilize or adapt habits which we acquired previously while learning some other language (generally the mother tongue) are more or less studial forms of work.

Most language-learners at the present day are found to make an almost exclusive use of their studial capacities, and in doing so use methods which are more or less unnatural.

3. *Why we must use our Studial Capacities*

We must not conclude from the foregoing that methods involving the use of our capacities for study are necessarily bad, nor that those based on our spontaneous capacities are necessarily always to be used. In certain cases and for certain purposes we shall be forced to use the former. Nature alone will not teach us how to read or write; for these purposes we must use our studial capacities. We shall, however, refrain from reading or writing any given material until we have learnt to use the spoken form. Nature will not teach us how to use forms of language which are not currently used in everyday speech; in order to acquire these we must have recourse to our powers of study; thus we shall use these powers when learning literary composition, the language of ceremony, etc. Moreover, the studial powers must be utilized for the purposes for which a *corrective course* is designed. What has been badly assimilated must be eliminated consciously; bad habits can only be replaced by good habits through processes unknown to the language-teaching forces of nature. Even those who have not been previously spoiled by defective study require a certain amount of corrective work in order that they may react against the tendency to import into the new language some or the characteristic features of the previously acquired language or languages.

Some students have no desire to *use* the foreign language, but merely wish to learn about it, to know something of its structure. In such cases no attempt whatever need be made to develop or to utilize their spontaneous language-learning capacities; they may work exclusively by the methods of study.

4. *The Student and his Aim*

We cannot design a language course until we know something about the students for whom the course is intended, for a programme of study depends on the aim or aims of the students. All we can say in advance is that we must endeavour to utilize the most appropriate means to attain the desired end. A course which is suitable in one case may prove unsuitable in another. Some students may require only a knowledge of the written language, others are concerned with the spoken language, others desire to become conversant with both aspects. Some students only require a superficial knowledge, while others aim at a perfect knowledge. Special categories of learners (e.g. clerks, hotel-keepers, tourists, grammarians) wish to specialize. The sole aim of some students is to pass a given examination; others wish to become proficient as translators or interpreters.

The length of the course or programme is a most important determining factor; a two months' course will differ fundamentally from one which is designed to last two years; the former will be a preparatory course, the latter will be highly developed.

It will not be possible for us to design a special course for each individual, still less to write a special textbook for him; we can, however, broadly group our students into types, and recommend for each type the most appropriate forms of work.

In any case, the teacher is bound to draw up some sort of programme in advance and to divide this into stages appropriately graded. This programme must not be of the rigid type, the same for all requirements; it should be designed on an elastic basis and should be in accordance with known pedagogical principles.

5. *The Supreme Importance of the Elementary Stage*

The reader of this book may notice, perhaps with some surprise, how much we have to say concerning the work of the beginner, and how little we say about the more advanced work; he may be puzzled at the amount of attention we pay to (what he may consider) crude elementary work compared with the amount we give to (what he may consider) the more complex and interesting work connected with the higher stages.

Language-study is essentially a habit-forming process, and the important stage in habit-forming is the elementary stage. If we do not secure habits of accurate observation, reproduction, and imitation during the first stage, it is doubtful whether we shall ever secure them subsequently. It is more difficult to unlearn a thing than to learn it. If the elementary stage is gone through without due regard to the principles of study, the student will be caused to do things which he must subsequently undo; he will acquire habits which will have to be eradicated. If his ear-training is neglected during the elementary stage, he will replace foreign sounds by native ones and insert intrusive sounds into the words of the language he is learning; he will become unable to receive any but eye-impressions, and so will become the dupe of unphonetic orthographies. If he has not been trained during the elementary stage to cultivate his powers of unconscious assimilation and reproduction, he will attempt the hopeless task of passing all the language-matter through the channel of full consciousness. If during the elementary stage he forms the 'isolating habit', he will not be able to use or to build accurate sentences. An abuse of translation during the elementary stage will cause the student to translate mentally everything he hears, reads, says, or writes. Bad habits of articulation will cause him to use language of an artificialized type.

The function of the elementary stage is to inculcate good habits, and once this work is done there is little or no fear of the student going astray in his later work. If we take care of the elementary stage, the advanced stage will take care of itself.

6. *The Principles of Language-Teaching*

The art of designing a language course appears to be in its infancy. Those arts which have achieved maturity have gradually evolved from a number of distinct primitive efforts which, by a process of gradual convergence towards each other, have resulted in the ideal type. So will it be in the art of composing language courses: the present diverse types will gradually be replaced by more general types, and in the end the ideal type will be evolved. This will come about as a result of a system of collaboration in which each worker will profit by that which has been done in the past and that which is being done by other workers in the present. Unsound methods will gradually be eliminated and will make room for methods which are being evolved slowly and experimentally and which will pass the tests of experience. By this time a series of essential principles will have been discovered, and these will be recognized as standard principles by all whose work is to design language courses.

The following list would seem to embody some of these, and probably represents principles on which there is general agreement among those who have made a study of the subject:

(1) The initial preparation of the student by the training of his spontaneous capacities for assimilating spoken language.

(2) The forming of new and appropriate habits and the utilization of previously formed habits.

131

(3) Accuracy in work in order to prevent the acquiring of bad habits.

(4) Gradation of the work in such a way as to ensure an ever-increasing rate of progress.

(5) Due proportion in the treatment of the various aspects and branches of the subject.

(6) The presentation of language-material in a concrete rather than in an abstract way.

(7) The securing and maintaining of the student's interest in order to accelerate his progress.

(8) A logical order of progression in accordance with principles of speech-psychology.

(9) The approaching of the subject simultaneously from different sides by means of different and appropriate devices.

7. Initial Preparation

We must realize that language-learning is an art, not a science. We may acquire proficiency in an art in two ways: by learning the theory, or by a process of imitation. This latter process is often termed the method of *trial and error*, but as the term may be misinterpreted it is better to consider it as the method of *practice*. The method of practice is a natural one, the method of theory is not. We may acquire proficiency in two ways: by forming appropriate new habits, or by utilizing and adapting appropriate old habits (i.e. habits already acquired). The natural process is the former, the latter being more or less artificial. Language-study is essentially a habit-forming process, so we must learn to form habits. By the natural or spontaneous method we learn unconsciously; we must therefore train ourselves or our students to form habits unconsciously.

The adult whose natural capacities for unconscious habit-forming have been dormant may reawaken them by means of appropriate exercises. These are notably:

(a) *Ear-training exercises*, by means of which he may learn to perceive correctly what he hears.

(*b*) *Articulation exercises*, by means of which he may cause his vocal organs to make the right sort of muscular efforts.

(*c*) *Exercises in mimicry*, by means of which he will become able to imitate and reproduce successfully any word or string of words uttered by the native whose speech serves as model.

(The combination of the three foregoing types of exercises will result in the capacity for reproducing at first hearing a string of syllables, such as a sentence. The student will thereby become enabled to memorize unconsciously the *form* of speech.)

(*d*) *Exercises in immediate comprehension*, by means of which he will come to grasp without mental translation or analysis the general sense of what he hears.

(*e*) *Exercises in forming the right associations between words and their meanings*, by means of which he will become able to express his thoughts.

The combination of these five types of exercise will develop the student's capacity to use spoken language.

8. *Habit-forming and Habit-adapting*

Language-study is essentially a habit-forming process. We speak and understand automatically as the result of perfectly formed habits. No foreign word or sentence is really 'known' until the student can produce it automatically (i.e. without hesitation or conscious calculation). No one can understand by any process of calculation (e.g. translation or analysis) the language as spoken normally by the native. Few people (if any) have ever succeeded in speaking the language by a series of mental gymnastics; our progress is to be measured only by the quantity of language-material which we can use automatically. Adult students generally dislike the work of acquiring new habits, and seek to replace it by forms of study dependent upon the intellect, striving to justify their abstention from mechanical work on educational grounds. This fear of tediousness is really groundless; automatism is certainly acquired by repetition, but this need not be of the monotonous, parrot-like type, for there exist many psychologically sound repetition devices and varied drills intended to ensure automatism and interest.

Most of the time spent by the teacher in demonstrating *why* a foreign sentence is constructed in a particular way is time wasted; it is generally enough for the student to learn to do things without learning why he must do them (due exception being made in special cases, notably that of corrective courses).

The student should not only be caused to form new habits; he should also be helped, when expedient, to utilize some of his existing habits; it is even part of the teacher's duties to aid the student to select from his previously acquired habits those which are likely to be of service to him.

9. *Accuracy*

Accuracy means *conformity with a given model or standard*, whatever that model or standard may happen to be. If we choose to take colloquial French or colloquial English as our standard, the forms pertaining to classical French or English (i.e. traditionally correct forms) are to be rejected as inaccurate. There are two types of inaccuracy: that in which a colloquial form is replaced by a classical form and *vice versa*, and that in which a native form is replaced by a pidgin form. In both cases the teacher's duty is to react against the tendency towards inaccuracy.

Appropriate drills and exercises exist which ensure accuracy in sounds, stress, intonation, fluency, spelling, sentence-building and compounding, inflexions, and meanings.

The principle of accuracy requires that *the student shall have no opportunities for making mistakes until he has arrived at the stage at which accurate work is reasonably to be expected.*

If we compel a student to utter foreign words before he has learnt how to make the requisite foreign sounds, if we compel him to write a composition in a foreign language before he has become reasonably proficient in sentence-building, or if we compel him to talk to us in the foreign language before he has done the necessary drill-work, we are compelling him to use the pidgin form of the language.

In addition to specific exercises and devices which ensure accuracy in special points, we should observe certain general rules which are described and treated under the heading of gradation.

10. *Gradation*

Gradation means passing from the known to the unknown by stages, each of which serves as a preparation for the next. If a course or a lesson is insufficiently graded, or graded on a wrong basis, the student's work will be marked by an excessive degree of inaccuracy. If a course is well graded, the student's rate of progress will increase in proportion as he advances.

In the ideally graded course the student is caused to assimilate perfectly a relatively small but exceedingly important vocabulary; when perfectly assimilated, this nucleus will develop and grow in the manner of a snowball.

Care should be taken to distinguish between false grading and sound grading. The following applications of this principle are psychologically sound:

(*a*) *Ears before Eyes.* The student to be given ample opportunities, at appropriate intervals, of hearing a sound, a word, or a group of words before seeing them in their written form (phonetic or other).

(*b*) *Reception before Reproduction.* The student to be given ample opportunities, with appropriate intervals, of hearing a sound or combination of sounds, a word, or a group of words before being called upon to imitate what he hears.

(*c*) *Oral Repetition before Reading.* The student to be given ample opportunities of repeating matter after the teacher before being called upon to read the same matter.

(*d*) *Immediate Memory before Prolonged Memory.* The student should not be required to reproduce matter heard a long time previously until he has become proficient in reproducing what he has just heard.

(*e*) *Chorus-work before Individual Work.* In the case of classes, new material should be repeated by the whole of the students together before each student is called upon to repeat individually. This will tend to ensure confidence.

(*f*) *Drill-work before Free Work.* The student should not be given opportunities for free conversation, free composition, or free translation until he has acquired a reasonable proficiency in the corresponding forms of drill-work.

Each individual item in the teaching should be graded, and in addition the whole course may be graded by dividing it into appropriate stages or phases, which will succeed each other *en échelon*.

11. *Proportion*

The ultimate aim of most students is fourfold:

(*a*) To understand what is said in the foreign language when it is spoken rapidly by natives.

(*b*) To speak the foreign language in the manner of natives.

(*c*) To understand the language as written by natives.

(*d*) To write the language in the manner of natives.

We observe the principle of proportion when we pay the right amount of attention to each of these four aspects, without exaggerating the importance of any of them.

There are five chief branches of practical linguistics:

(*a*) *Phonetics*, which teaches us to recognize and to reproduce sounds and tones.

(*b*) *Orthography*, which teaches us to spell what we have already learnt by ear.

(*c*) *Accidence and etymology*, which teaches us the nature of inflected forms and derivatives, and also how to use them.

(*d*) *Syntax and analysis*, which teaches us how to build up sentences from their components.

(*e*) *Semantics*, which teaches us the meanings of words and forms.

We observe the principle of proportion when we pay the right amount of attention to each of these five branches, without exaggerating the importance of any of them.

In choosing the units of our vocabulary we may be guided by several considerations, such as intrinsic utility, sentence-forming utility, grammatical function, regularity, facility, concreteness, or completeness. We observe the principle of proportion when we select the material of our vocabularies in such a way that due attention is paid to all such desiderata, and without exaggerating the importance of any of them.

We also observe the principle of proportion when we give the right amount of drill-work or free work, or translation-work or 'direct' work, of intensive reading or extensive reading. A well-proportioned course, like a well-graded course, ensures a steady and ever-increasing rate of progress.

12. *Concreteness*

We are enjoined by the principle of concreteness to teach more by example than by precept. When we give explanations we should illustrate these by striking and vivid examples embodying the point of theory which is the subject of our explanation. One example is generally not enough; it is by furnishing several examples bearing on the same point that we cause the student to grasp that which is common to them all.

But this is not enough: the examples themselves may vary in concreteness; therefore we should select for our purpose those which demonstrate in the clearest possible way the point we are teaching and which tend to form the closest semantic associations. We should utilize as far as possible the actual environment of the student: the grammar of the noun is best understood when we talk of books, pencils, and chairs; the grammar of the verb is best grasped when we choose as examples verbs

THE PRINCIPLES OF LANGUAGE-STUDY

which can be 'acted'; *black, white, round, square* are more concrete adjectives than *rich, poor, idle, diligent.*

There are four ways of teaching the meanings of words or forms:

(1) *By immediate association,* as when we point to the object represented by a noun.

(2) *By translation,* as when we give the student the nearest native equivalent.

(3) *By definition,* as when we describe the unit by means of a synonymous expression.

(4) *By context,* as when we embody the word or expression in a sentence which will make its meaning clear.

These four manners are given here in what is generally their order of concreteness; it is interesting to note in this connexion that translation is not nearly so 'indirect' or 'unconcrete' as the extreme 'direct methodists' have led us to suppose.

It is for the teacher to judge under what conditions each of these four manners of teaching meanings may be appropriately used.

13. *Interest*

No work is likely to be successfully accomplished if the student is not interested in what he is doing, but in our efforts to interest the pupil we must take care that the quality of the teaching does not suffer. Habit-forming work has the reputation of being dull and tedious. The remedy, however, would not be to abandon it in favour of work which in itself is or seems more interesting (such as reading, composition, and translation exercises), for by so doing we should merely be leaving undone work which must be done. The true remedy is to devise a number of varied and appropriate exercises in order to make the habit-forming work itself interesting.

The most ingenious and interesting arithmetical problems alone will not assist the student in memorizing the multiplication table, and the most ingenious and interesting sentence-building devices alone will not cause the student to obtain the necessary automatic command of the fundamental material of the language.

There are notably six factors making for interest (and the observing of these will not in any appreciable degree violate the eight other principles involved), viz.:

(1) *The Elimination of Bewilderment.* Difficulty is one thing: bewilderment is another. The student must, in the ordinary course of events, be confronted with difficulties, but he should never be faced with hopeless puzzles. Rational explanations and good grading will eliminate bewilderment and, in so doing, will tend to make the course interesting.

(2) *The Sense of Progress achieved.* When the student feels that he is making progress, he will rarely fail to be interested in his work.

(3) *Competition.* The spirit of emulation adds zest to all study.

(4) *Game-like Exercises.* Many forms of exercise so resemble games of skill that they are often considered as interesting as chess and similar pastimes.

(5) *The Relation between Teacher and Student.* The right attitude of the teacher towards his pupils will contribute largely towards the interest taken in the work.

(6) *Variety.* Change of work generally adds interest: an alternation of different sorts of monotonous work makes the whole work less monotonous. Spells of drill-work, however, should be relieved by intervals devoted to work of a less monotonous character.

14. *A Rational Order of Progression*

Apart from all questions of grading, we may observe in most of the branches of language-work different orders of progression. We may proceed from the spoken to the written or from the written to the spoken: we may start with ear-training and articulation exercises or leave them to a later stage: we may treat intonation as a fundamental or leave it to the final stage: we may proceed from the sentence to the word or *vice versa*: irregularities may be included or excluded during the first part of the course: we may proceed from rapid and fluent to slow utterance or *vice versa*.

Modern pedagogy tends to favour the former of each of these alternatives: whereas the teachers of the past generations generally pronounced in favour of the latter. The ancient school said: First learn how to form words, then learn how to form sentences, then pay attention to the 'idiomatic' phenomena, and lastly learn how to pronounce and to speak. The modern school says: First learn to form sounds, then memorize sentences, then learn systematically how to form sentences, and lastly learn how to form words.

The two orders of progression, it will be seen, are almost directly opposite to each other. We who have carefully examined and analysed the arguments on either side are forced to conclude that the modern order is the rational order, and psychologists will confirm our conclusion. The old order stands for cramming and for an erratic and weak curve of progress: the modern order stands for results which are both immediate and of a permanent nature. The old order teaches us much about the language and its theory: the modern order teaches us how to *use* a language.

15. *The Multiple Line of Approach*

This ninth and last of the essential principles of language-study welds the eight others into a consistent whole; it harmonizes any seeming contradictions and enables us to observe in a perfectly rational manner all of the precepts set forth under their respective headings; it answers once for all most of those perplexing questions which have engaged the attention of so many language-teachers and controversialists for such a long time.

If this principle is in contradiction to the spirit of partisanship, it is equally opposed to the spirit of compromise; it suggests a third and better course, that of accepting any two or more rival expedients and of embodying them boldly as separate items in the programme, in order that each may fulfil its function in a well-proportioned and well-organized whole.

The term 'multiple line of approach' implies that we are to proceed simultaneously from many different starting-points towards one and the same end; we use each and every method, process, exercise, drill, or device which may further us in our immediate purpose and bring us nearer to our ultimate goal; we adopt every good idea and leave the door open for all future developments; we reject nothing except useless and harmful forms of work. The multiple line of approach embodies the eclectic principle (using the term in its general and favourable sense), for it enjoins us to select judiciously and without prejudice all that is likely to help us in our work. Whether our purpose is the complete mastery of the language in all its aspects and branches, or whether our purpose is a more special one, the principle holds good: we adopt the best and most appropriate means towards the required end.

16. 'Memorized Matter' and 'Constructed Matter'

When more is known about speech-psychology and the ultimate process of language-study, it will be possible to embody as one of the fundamental principles the following considerations:

The whole of our speech-material is possessed by us either as 'memorized matter' or as 'constructed matter'.

Memorized matter includes everything which we have memorized integrally, whether syllables, words, word-groups, sentences, or whole passages.

Constructed matter includes everything not so memorized, i.e. matter which we compose as we go on, matter which we build up unit by unit from our stock of memorized matter while we are speaking or writing.

There are three manners of producing constructed matter

from memorized matter; we may term these respectively *grammatical construction, ergonic construction,* and *conversion.*

Grammatical Construction. In this process, our memorized matter consists of '*dictionary words*' (i.e. uninflected and unmodified root-like words). By learning the theories of accidence, syntax, derivation, and composition we become (or hope to become) able to produce constructed matter at will.

Ergonic Construction. In this process, our memorized matter consists of two elements: *more or less complete sentences and 'working words*' (units of speech ready inflected, ready modified, ready derived, or ready compounded), which units may be termed 'ergons'. By means of appropriate tables and drill-like forms of work, from this memorized matter we produce more or less spontaneously the requisite constructed matter.

Conversion. In this process, our memorized matter consists of classified series of sentences which are to be converted into other forms by means of appropriate exercises of various kinds.

In the opinion of many, the greatest evil in present-day methods lies in the fact that an almost exclusive use is made of the first of these processes as a method of producing constructed matter. Instead of concentrating their efforts on condemning this process as a vicious and unnatural one, the reformers of thirty years ago merely advocated what has been termed the 'direct method', the chief features of which are the abolition of translation exercises and of the use of the mother tongue as a vehicle of instruction.

2010
2013